Ghosts of
North-West England

Peter Underwood

Ghosts of
North-West England

Peter Underwood has been President of The Ghost Club (founded 1862) since 1960 and has probably heard more first-hand ghost stories than any man alive. A long-standing member of The Society for Psychical Research, Vice-President of the Unitarian Society for Psychical Studies, a member of The Folklore Society, The Dracula Society and a former member of the Research Committee of the Psychic Research Organization, he has lectured, written and broadcast extensively. He took part in the first official investigation into a haunting; has sat with physical and mental mediums and conducted investigations at seances, been present at exorcisms, experiments at dowsing, precognition, clairvoyance, hypnotism, regression; conducted world-wide tests in telepathy and extra-sensory perception, and has personally investigated scores of haunted houses. He possesses comprehensive files of alleged hauntings in every county of the British Isles and many foreign countries, and his knowledge and experience has resulted in his being consulted on psychic and occult matters by the BBC and ITV. Literary Executor to the Harry Price Estate since 1974, his many books include the first two comprehensive gazetteers of ghosts and hauntings in England, Scotland and Ireland and two books that deal with twenty different occult subjects. He selected and edited with an Introduction, *Thirteen Famous Ghost Stories* for Dents Everyman's Library (1977) and his *Hauntings* (1977) re-examines ten classic cases of haunting in the light of modern knowledge. Born at Letchworth Garden City in Hertfordshire, he now lives in a small village in Hampshire. He is Hon. Librarian of The Savage Club, 9 Fitzmaurice Place, Berkeley Square, London, W1, where he can be contacted.

First published in Fontana Paperbacks 1978

Copyright © Peter Underwood 1978

CONDITIONS OF SALE
This book is sold subject to the condition that
it shall not, by way of trade or otherwise, be lent,
re-sold, hired out or otherwise circulated without
the publisher's prior consent in any form of
binding or cover other than that in which it is
published and without a similar condition
including this condition being imposed on the
subsequent purchaser

*For our good friends
Freda and Steuart Kiernander of Buxton
who, over the years, have made all our
visits treasured memories*

CONTENTS

Introduction

A-Z   p.9

Illustrations   p.215

Index   p.225

Introduction

Dr Samuel Johnson considered the subject of ghosts to be 'one of the most important that can come before the human understanding ... a question which, after five thousand years, is yet undecided ...' I hardly expect this modest volume, containing only a small number of the reported ghosts in a small area of Britain, to decide the matter one way or the other; indeed my experience is that few people believe in ghosts until they see one. Nevertheless, this collection, incomplete and of varying quality as it may be, represents a fascinating cross-section of human experience and belief.

Here are first-hand accounts of haunted houses, halls, inns and rectories; haunted lakes, ruins and open spaces; haunted hospitals and cinemas and theatres; stories of haunted skulls, a haunted taxi-cab, a ghostly footprint ... modern ghosts and traditional hauntings, some which I mention briefly while others are related at some length. Together these true stories reveal a richer harvest of strange experience than I had dared to hope when I set out to compile this book.

I am deeply grateful to everyone who has helped me along the way: to my wife Joyce who has accompanied me in my search for ghosts, many hundreds of miles for this volume alone; to our good friends Freda and Steuart Kiernander, to whom I dedicate this volume; to all the librarians, public officials and private individuals who have so generously and courteously helped me with my unending enquiries and I feel that I must especially mention: W. D. Amos, Editor of *Lancashire Life*; Michael Bingham of Pakuranga, New Zealand; Vera Bottomley of Stalybridge; Michael Brett of Coppenhall, Crewe; Lt. Col. Sir Walter Bromley-Davenport of Capesthorne Hall; Olive Carson of Chester; Cyril Dickinson and the *Wigan Observer*; Betty and Freda Driver; Canon Wilfrid Garlick of

Stockport; Viscountess Garnock of Combermere Abbey; Alex Grant, Chairman of Kirkby Local History Society; Derek and Hazel Hanson and Arthur and Margaret Cheetham of Formby; Mrs Maynard Howarth of Chingle Hall; Dr Peter Hilton-Rowe of Dedham; Ken Howarth, Museum Assistant at Bury; Colonel Roger Fleetwood Hesketh of Meols Hall; Miss C. Jones of Wrexham; P.W.G. Lawson, Curator of Speke Hall; W.B. Leeming, Divisional Librarian of Warrington; Colin J. Lynch of Northwich; Denis E. Mather of Swillbrook; Tom Perrott, Chairman of the Ghost Club; H.B. Ratcliffe, Curator of Ruffold Old Hall; Raymond and Monica Richards of Gawsworth Hall; Stewart Rigby and the *Stockport Express*; Rev. Francis J. Ripley of Ashton-in-Makerfield; Jim Sharratt of Up Holland; the Rev. Alan Shone of Rochdale; Malcolm Smith of Appley Bridge; Mary Stanley of the *Birkenhead News*; D.R. Stockley and the Spontaneous Phenomena Research Unit; Wilfred Tattum, former superintendent at St. Thomas's Hospital, Stockport; Colonel R.T. Turner of Thurstaston Hall; Albert and Doris Walker, Custodians of Turton Tower; all the friendly and helpful people from the North West and my publishers for the opportunity of doing the book.

Having reached the end of this book I shall miss, hopefully only for a little while, the warmth and kindness of the people of the north west of England but my lifetime search for ghosts and haunted houses still continues and I am always pleased to hear from anyone with information on this absorbing subject.

The Savage Club PETER UNDERWOOD
Fitzmaurice Place
Berkeley Square
London, W1

Accrington, LANCASHIRE

Accrington has several ghosts, some ancient and some modern. Perhaps the oldest goes back to the time when the neighbourhood of Black Abbey was fresh and sweet; then the monastic establishment that gave the area its name flourished and the monks lived their jovial and contented lives, but one brother fell in love with a local damsel and knowing all too well the penalties for such an affair, they kept their trysting a secret, often using a room in one of the towers of the Black Abbey as their meeting place. Inevitably perhaps, the girl's father discovered what was happening and one night when the lovers were together the father forced his way into the room where they were. The monk hurriedly pushed his sweetheart into a secret passage and then met her father with stolid indifference and would give no answer to his questions about his daughter.

The enraged father aroused the brethren of the abbey, who seized the monk and put him in chains. They then sealed the door and set fire to the tower. As the monk lay helpless he heard his sweetheart's voice and she returned from the secret compartment to the burning room. She was unable to release him and he beseeched her to escape through the passage but she put her arms about him and said they would die together. In the morning their charred remains were found under the debris of the burnt-out tower and, according to local legend, at midnight on pitch-black, moonless nights, an arresting sight is re-enacted at the spot where the tower once stood.

A luminous figure of a beautiful young maiden emerges from the site of the Black Abbey, her long golden tresses blowing in the breeze, her lovely features marred by an inexpressible sadness. She is dressed in a white robe, fastened with a girdle about the waist and her right arm is withered and fleshless as though scorched and burnt by flames.

Uttering a piercing shriek that strikes terror into any witness of the visitation, the ghost disappears.

When the district of Peel Park consisted merely of a few small cottages, a former occupant of one was a miser known as 'Old Ailse'. After her death many searches failed to reveal the hiding place of her wealth; it was said that her spirit could not rest and there were persistent stories of people seeing the form of a little old lady hurrying hither and thither and then disappearing inexplicably.

When a portion of the once lordly mansion of Accrington Hall, the residence of Jonathan Peel, came to be built on, the site of the cottage once occupied by 'Old Ailse' was excavated and her secret hoard is said to have been discovered and thereafter her ghost was seen no more.

A similar story is told concerning a ghost that once haunted some old property that used to occupy the site of the shops at the corner of Blackburn Road and Abbey Street. Tasker Street runs behind and this was formerly a road that was called Tit-tat Lane. An old farm occupied the corner of Barnes Street, opposite, which existed prior to Abbey Street being built. The ghost is said to have been that of an old miser who also died without disclosing where he had hidden his wealth and his ghost walked, usually at night, in and around his old home until the property was demolished. The contractor who was responsible for pulling the property down is said to have found the miser's gold. An old inhabitant, the late William Ashworth, lived nearby as a boy and heard this story related to him many times as the solemn truth. As proof, he was told the contractor 'never looked back' after demolishing the old miser's house.

Accrington also had a haunted cinema. The Classic on Broadway was the scene of some curious happenings in November, 1973, when an Irish workman, John Murphy, said a pair of ghostly, cold and clammy hands went up the nape of his neck and pulled his head back. He raced out of the ballroom bar that was being renovated and would never go back. A workmate said John was a 'pretty hard-boiled, down-to-earth sort of chap . . . he must have felt something to get so upset.'

The cinema manager, Mr Sidney Gournell, stated that he had experienced a number of odd occurrences including one occasion when the screen curtains were suddenly drawn across the screen during the showing of a film. At first he thought one of the staff had either made a mistake or was having a joke but it seems that no one had been responsible and the incident remained a mystery. On another occasion Sidney Gournell saw a 'curious dark shadow' in the shape of a man of below-medium height in an upstairs room; a few minutes later the 'shadow' had disappeared. Mysterious blue lights have been seen in certain corridors and the cinema cat was apparently affected at one time. Normally a very placid creature, when the 'ghostly' happenings occurred the animal seemed to go wild and started charging about all over the place.

Altrincham, GREATER MANCHESTER

The Studio One cinema is reputed to be haunted by the ghost of a young man who hanged himself in the orchestra pit when the place was the Hippodrome Theatre and although Frank Hargreaves, grandson of the building's founder, points to the improbability of the suicide story – and it certainly would appear to be a difficult feat in the present situation – stories of strange happenings have emanated from the building for many years now.

The noises and sensations always seem to take place when the building is empty and the public have left; it is then that locked doors are heard to creak and slowly open, footfalls are heard walking along deserted corridors and climbing empty stairways and a frightening coldness and the impression of a presence has been repeatedly noticed in the projection room. Indeed most of the reports of unusual events appear to centre around the projection room, so perhaps the story of the location of the suicide has become confused and the place where the young man died was in fact the projection room of the haunted cinema.

After working at the cinema for several years as chief and assistant technician respectively, Dave Grant and Philip Drinkwater have become accustomed to the mysterious events. Dave repeatedly has found 'a kind of shadow' distracting his attention when in the projection room, watching the film through one of the viewing windows. The shadow moves backwards and forwards behind him. He can sense it, yet when he turns round there is nobody there. His assistant has experienced the same thing on numerous occasions over the years. 'It doesn't worry me any more,' Philip Drinkwater said in June, 1975. 'It's just annoying, really.'

In 1972, however, Philip had a more frightening experience. He was on his own in the projection room when he suddenly became aware that there was someone, or something, behind him. Thinking it was Dave, who was having his break, he called out 'Oh, you're back are you?' When no one answered he looked round and the room was completely empty. He was really shaken and afterwards refused to be in the room by himself.

Dave, when in the projection room on his own, has always been aware of some 'force' in the room with him. Once, working late after the film had ended and everywhere else was locked up, he heard the front doors swing open, then swing back and he heard footsteps climb the stairs. He immediately checked the whole building. There was no one anywhere and all the doors were closed and locked.

Dominic McSorley was manager of the cinema for nine months before he left in 1975 and he has no doubts about the building being haunted, and he believes he knows why. He found out that when the property was first built it provided live entertainment and the family who owned the theatre at that time were the Hargreaves of Rochdale. The youngest Hargreaves was stage manager but he always nursed the ambition of acting. The family flatly refused to consider the idea of his following such a low profession; it was bad enough that he insisted on working in the theatre. One night the sadness and frustration of it all overflowed and he hanged himself, possibly in the orchestra pit.

Thereafter any technical errors, faults, unexplained noises or strange happenings in the theatre were always put down by the staff to 'Old Hargreaves'. Certainly historical research has revealed that when the building opened in 1912, playing vaudeville, the Hargreaves family of Rochdale did indeed run the theatre; but there seems to be no record of a suicide. The local registrars have no record of a Hargreaves committing suicide in the theatre between 1910 and 1930, the year it changed from vaudeville to a picture house. But Dominic McSorley is not sure that this necessarily settles the matter. In those days money really talked and it is quite possible that a wealthy family could have hushed up such an affair.

Dominic himself has heard noises in the theatre that he is certain have no material origin. Once he heard cracking noises coming from the area of one of the radiator pipes but there was no oil in the theatre at the time and he is convinced that it was not the result of heating or cooling. At the same time some of the theatre seats that had been left in a raised position started to snap down; this can normally happen only if the spring is broken, and Dominic carefully checked a number of the seats that he saw go down and the springs were found to be in perfect order.

Other reported happenings have included: lights in two of the projectors switching themselves off for no apparent reason and both being subsequently found to be in good order; coloured lights found whirring away after they have been switched off the night before; the intercom system ringing for no good reason; and, occasionally, moaning noises being heard emanating from the empty projection room. Small wonder that Dominic McSorley is just one of the people who say, 'I did not believe in ghosts before I worked there . . .' but the strange happenings seem to come and go in phases; sometimes all is quiet for a while but before long 'Old Hargreaves', or whatever it is that haunts the cinema, returns to puzzle the manager and his staff.

Several roads in the Timperley area of Altrincham are apparently haunted by strange night sounds, according to readers of the local newspapers in June, 1976. Residents of both Sylvan Avenue and Riddings Road wrote to the *Altrincham Guardian* recounting strange happenings: John Pedley said that he and his brother had been hearing thuds on the lounge windows of their home at night, usually around ten or eleven o'clock. These did not seem to have any real pattern, merely occurring at random, once when John was alone in the house, sitting in a chair by the window watching television, at other times when his mother, Mrs Kathleen Pedley, has been alone in the house and when she has been too scared to try and see what has caused the heavy thuds. Sometimes, when they have both been in the house together, John has tried to find an explanation but he has never been successful. He has noticed that the thuds only seem to occur in the vicinity of two particular windows but the sounds have been heard on the calmest nights as well as windy ones. They sound exactly as though someone was throwing earth at the window, even being followed by sounds like earth falling, but there is never any trace of earth and never anyone near the window. John said in June 1976 that he and his mother had both become more aware of the noises during the previous twelve months.

Early one morning in 1971, Janet Ball was astonished to hear the sound of horses' hooves clattering sharply in the stillness outside the window of her home in Ashley Road, for the time was just after three o'clock. She had been out late that evening and had just got to bed when, first of all, she heard strange moaning noises coming from the street outside. Then she heard the sound of a coach and horses coming up the road. For some reason she felt terrified and she couldn't move or cry out; the whole of her body was stiff and she felt icy cold. The sounds passed the house and gradually died away in the distance.

Next day Janet went to her local library, determined to find out whether there was any historical reason for the sounds she had heard so plainly. There she discovered that Ashley Road had once been an old coaching road, frequented by horse-drawn coaches on their way to Dunham Park. In 1975 a neighbour of Janet's heard similar sounds, including the moaning noises, late one night.

Appley Bridge, near Wigan, GREATER MANCHESTER

A discoloured human skull is kept on a beam in the living-room at the quaint old Skull House, a human relic that is reputed to promote ill-luck and unwelcome disturbances if it is taken out of the house.

No one seems to know to whom the skull belonged, for it has been at Skull House so long that historians and other people interested in the mystery think it is now unlikely that the past will ever unfold its secret.

Over the years the various inhabitants of the house have treated the skull with varying degrees of respect and affection. Mrs E. A. Unsworth was at Skull House for a quarter of a century and with contemptuous disregard for its legendary bad luck to those who handled it, she kept it behind the old-fashioned fireplace and brought it out of its cardboard box and showed it to anyone who was interested. Mrs Unsworth scoffed at the idea of the skull having the power to promote happenings and she refused to believe that the house was haunted although it has that tradition. She used to say that some people said it was the skull of a monk who had been beheaded in an upstairs room at Skull House while others thought it had belonged to a knight who was killed nearby.

It is a strange house, full of walls riddled with mysterious cupboards; chimneys that lead goodness knows where; leaded windows decorated with skulls; a door more than four hundred years old; low ceilings; massive beams; odd corners and nooks and crannies; a priest's hole; a hollow beam and boarded-up underground cellars.

In 1937 one investigator dug up the legend of the monk that could explain the presence of the skull. It seems that at the time that Cromwell's Ironsides were ravaging the countryside hereabouts a priest, closely pursued by a couple of Roundheads, fled to Skull House and, in an effort to escape, climbed up the broad chimney to hide in the small room which can still be reached from one of the bedrooms. Cromwell's men promptly made a huge fire in the grate and before long, overcome by the fumes, the priest was forced to surrender and he was immediately beheaded. The skull is said to be his and the rest of his body may well lie buried in the garden or be hidden somewhere within the rabbit-warren of a house. Unfortunately for this theory, historians say Cromwell's men never reached Wigan and medical evidence leans towards the skull being female!

Another occupant, Mrs H. Lee, who lived at Skull House with her husband and their two sons, used to repeat another legend, that the skull belonged to a knight who lived in the days of King Arthur. This story says that about the year 1500 there were four knights in a house on the site of Skull House, one of whom was known as The Knight of the Death's Head or The Knight of the Skull, from his practice of wearing a human skull on top of his helmet to frighten his enemies. This was the knight Tennyson mentioned in his epic 'Sir Gareth and Lynette', where he says Sir Gareth had to overcome the Knight of the Skull before winning Castle Dangerous. It is an interesting fact that near to Skull House is a place named Dangerous Corner. The Old English word for 'corner' is 'cantle' and this could easily have been mistaken over the years for 'castle'. It is also interesting to remember that there have always been students of Arthurian lore and legend who believe that while King Arthur and his Knights may have come from Somerset, there is the strong possibility that he had headquarters in Lancashire and even fought battles along the banks of the River Douglas where, it has been suggested, the skull was found.

Legend has always said that ill-fortune will follow anyone who takes the skull from Skull House and that, anyway, the skull will return by itself. Once it is said to have been thrown into the nearby river but it found its way back to the house.

In February 1977 Mr Malcolm Smith, the present occupant, told me: 'We have lived here for seven years but haven't encountered any ghostly happenings yet!'

Ashton-under-Lyne, GREATER MANCHESTER

A house in Philip Avenue, Audenshaw, was reported to become suddenly haunted in 1971 when, in the room that he shared with his four-year-old brother Graham, Trevor Hulley, aged six, found himself awake between 12.30 and one o'clock in the morning, shivering, crying and terribly frightened. Mrs Hulley decided he must have had a nightmare and she took him into her bed. Meanwhile Graham turned over and tried to go back to sleep but ten minutes later Mrs Hulley heard a scream from the boys' bedroom and she found Graham shaking with fear and as cold as ice. He said that his brother Trevor had been very frightened, saying he kept seeing things and crying and keeping him awake. When their mother had taken him out of the room Graham had tried to go back to sleep but the room had become colder and colder and then, down at the bottom of his bed he saw his Gran (paternal grandmother) standing, waving and inviting him to go with her. She was wearing a long white gown and he was surprised to see that she wasn't wearing her spectacles; he had never seen her without spectacles. He could see the wedding ring on her finger and a big scar down the side of her face. He knew there was something odd about the figure and he screamed and then his Grandad appeared with Nanna (maternal grandmother) and they led Gran away, holding her hand. They went through the wall; the boy added that his Grandfather waved to him just as he disappeared.

Graham's Grandfather died two years earlier when Graham was only two years old and yet the boy immediately recognized his Grandfather and described him as looking like his own father and his uncle and indeed the family say there is a striking resemblance. The boys' Grandmother died only six months before he saw her ghost. She had been involved in an accident before her death and her face was bandaged up to the time of her death so that Graham had never seen the scar. He described the long white gown that she was wearing when she was buried and the fact that her glasses were missing. Both the boys' parents agreed that on the night in question the boys' room did seem to be unnaturally cold.

Bartle, near Preston, LANCASHIRE

Swillbrook House, a solidly built structure that dates back to Elizabethan times, stands in extensive grounds and is now the home of genial Denis G. Mather and his family. The haunting at Swillbrook is also said to date back many years and to involve a jealous husband who set a trap for his faithless wife. With great cunning and greater secrecy he arranged a pair of swords beneath his wife's bed in such a way that they would pierce the mattress and kill the guilty pair as they sported with each other . . . unfortunately the only child of the family found her way into the bedroom and during play, bounced up and down on the bed; the cleverly placed swords did their work and the child was fatally injured.

The 'haunted room' is now Denis Mather's main guestroom and none of his guests have ever reported sleepless nights or visitation from ghosts but perhaps the charming personalities of the present occupants of Swillbrook House have laid for ever the unhappy ghosts of yesteryear.

As he showed my wife and me over his delightful home Denis Mather told us he had been there ten years and had never seen or heard anything he could not explain but his mother, who often stayed at the house, said she occasionally heard footsteps in the corridor between her room and the 'haunted room' and also a noise she described as resembling a rocking chair in motion – it immediately occurred to me that this noise could possibly be associated with the traditional haunting that is concerned with a form or forms that bounce on the very comfortable-looking bedstead in the 'haunted room'. Local people certainly consider Swillbrook House to be haunted and there have been recent instances of local girls refusing to come and work at the house because of its reputation. We gathered that our host rather liked the *idea* of his house being haunted.

Barton-on-Irwell, LANCASHIRE

Ye Old Rock House inn is reputed to have a ghost that survived the rebuilding of the place in the 1920s: the ghost of a man who looks like a country yokel. In fact, according to tradition, it is a member of the de Trafford family.

During the Civil War the Roundheads were seeking out the Royalist de Traffords and the son of the family, on an impulse, tore off his clothing, put on a servant's smock, snatched up a flail and busied himself threshing corn in a barn with a couple of manservants. Cromwell's men were looking for gentry and they spared no more than a brief glance at the three workmen muttering together in the dusty barn.

As with so many legends there may well be a modicum of truth in this one, for not many years ago, under the floor of the attic, a flail and a pile of mouldy garments were uncovered and the flail and a few buttons (the clothing disintegrated when exposed to the air) serve as physical remains of a ghost that is still seen from time to time, although why this should be so is not known, unless, contrary to legend, the young de Trafford was caught and put to death by the crafty Roundheads.

Bickerstaffe, near Ormskirk, LANCASHIRE

Mossock Hall Farm was Mossock Hall two hundred years ago, an impressive structure with mullioned windows and massive chimneys. The origin of the ghostly Green Lady that haunted the house for a hundred and fifty years is lost in antiquity and so are the circumstances surrounding a second ghost that was always seen at the foot of the great staircase, seemingly searching for something – long-lost treasure perhaps?

Billinge, near St Helens, MERSEYSIDE

The Stork Hotel, originally built as a jail and used as such by Cromwell, dates from 1640 and it was in an underground chamber, now part of the cellars, that a Royalist prisoner is said to have died in suspicious circumstances. His ghost now haunts the hotel.

The area is also reputed to be haunted by a ghostly horse and rider that gallops through Billinge after midnight. Sounds of cantering horses have been heard many times when no animals are visible. One early morning motor-cyclist also saw the mounted phantom.

George Sadler, the licensee in 1972, revealed that a customer had recently claimed to have seen the ghostly cavalier. He had been washing his hands in the gents when he looked up and saw 'a fancy chap' standing beside him. He thought there must be a fancy dress party going on somewhere and he subsequently asked about it. The customer came from Leeds and knew nothing about the reputed haunting of the premises by a cavalier.

Heavy footsteps that have no natural origin have been heard by many people in the bar. The sounds appear to come from the floor above while anyone in the room above at the time feels that the footsteps come from the room below. On occasions the ghost footsteps have been loud enough to awaken guests, as they did in August 1972.

Bispham Hall at Billinge is also reputed to be haunted. The rambling sixteenth-century house was built by the Bispham family but is now used as a Boy Scout headquarters. A ghostly white dog has been reported, in daylight, in the vicinity of a dog's grave and many Scouts have been puzzled by inexplicable lights.

Birkenhead, MERSEYSIDE

An old house in Canning Street is now used by a contractor for storage purposes; once it was so badly haunted by the ghost of a sailor that several families left the property because they had seen the ghost and were convinced that the place was haunted. My account is based on the story related by Margaret Stanley in the *Birkenhead News* of 19 March, 1975.

The house used to be called 'Waters Edge' and when it was newly occupied by a sea captain and his young wife, they employed a responsible and sensible Yorkshirewoman as cook and housekeeper. She was told that they would also be having a nurse temporarily living in as his wife was expecting her first baby. The night the new housekeeper arrived she was unpacking and settling into her room, situated at the top of the house, when she heard someone come out of the room next to hers and go down the stairs. She thought nothing of the matter and was soon in bed but, although she was tired after her journey, she slept little and already felt there was something strange about the house.

Next day the housekeeper talked at some length with her employer and learned that the nurse would be arriving shortly and that the Captain was away at sea, but was expected home within a few days. Gradually the housekeeper settled down but from time to time she heard the sounds of someone in the room next to hers, as well as footsteps in the passageway and descending the stairs. She said nothing to her employer because of her condition and then, in a couple of days, the nurse arrived and was installed in a room near to the expectant mother on the first floor of the house.

One evening the housekeeper was in her sitting-room on the ground floor, quietly reading, when she suddenly felt that someone had come into the room. She glanced round at the door and it was closed (as she had left it) but still she had the definite impression that someone was in the room with her and she sensed that this 'person' came quite close to her for a moment and then passed into the kitchen and out into the garden. Putting out the light, the housekeeper went up to her bedroom. Chancing to encounter the nurse on the way and feeling that she must tell someone about the incidents she had experienced, she related what had happened, both in the bedroom and in the downstairs sitting-room. The nurse was slightly incredulous but sympathetic and told the housekeeper not to hesitate to come to her room at any time if she felt she needed help.

On the night that the baby was born the nurse left the mother and child for a moment to fetch something from her room and as she walked out on to the landing she saw the figure of a man coming slowly down the stairs from the top floor of the house. She looked at him in astonishment for she was under the impression that there was no man in the house. The man she saw was obviously a seaman although his clothing seemed strangely old-fashioned. His face was in shadow and he passed her and continued on down the stairs to the ground floor.

Next morning she casually asked her charge whether her husband was already home, to which her employer replied in the negative, followed by the question, 'Why do you ask?' The nurse then related what she had seen but the description in no way fitted her employer's husband and, having been told that she must have been mistaken, the nurse dropped the subject.

About a week later the housekeeper, who in the meantime had several times experienced the disturbing sensation of someone invisible being about the house, told her employer that she did not feel comfortable in the house and had decided to leave as soon as possible. As it happened the Captain returned the following day and his wife related what she had been told by the nurse and the housekeeper.

Next morning the Captain called on the estate agent through whom he had obtained the house and, when he related what he had been told, they admitted that there had been similar stories from several other tenants who had left the house after occupying it for short periods. One of the partners in the business was sufficiently interested in the matter to suggest that he and the Captain sit up that night and see whether they could find out for themselves what was happening. The Captain agreed and they both sat up all night but had nothing to report in the morning.

They agreed to try one more night and this time they were more successful. In the middle of the night they heard the creak of floorboards, followed by unmistakable footsteps and looking up they both saw the figure of a man walking down the stairs from the top part of the house towards them. He was dressed in the costume of a sailor, but a sailor of bygone days, and he appeared to be completely solid; walking firmly but slowly he passed them and they followed him down the stairs to the ground floor, through into the kitchen and then out into the back garden. There they waited and watched from the shelter of the back door as he made his unhurried way almost to the bottom of the garden and then suddenly he was no longer there.

The Captain had seen enough and he moved his family out of the house shortly afterwards. When she wrote her piece about the haunting, Margaret Stanley tried to discover whether anything odd or unusual had been discovered when the garden was converted into a parking space for the contractor's vehicles, but in this she was unsuccessful.

At the end of 1976, a macabre apparition struck such terror into a family living in Paterson Street that the four children, aged sixteen, twelve and two of five at the time, refused to go upstairs. At first the trouble was confined to noises: odd coughing and choking sounds that seemed to follow the family about the terraced house and subsequently the form of a tall hanging man was seen near the banister.

When they were younger the little girl twins obviously saw the same sinister form, later seen by the rest of the family, for they would look up the stairs and say 'man – man'. Then they would start screaming and say 'man gone – man gone'. Their mother explained that they were frightened by what they saw; they just couldn't understand what was happening when the form disappeared, and perhaps because the figure seemed to be so tall.

A bell, book and candle ceremony by a local priest had no effect but this clergyman made some enquiries and discovered that years earlier a tall man, over six feet four inches in height, was in fact found hanging from the banister of the house. Apparently the body had been there about four days before it was discovered.

Nor was it only the family who saw this figure; Mrs Josie Mearnd, the children's mother, said at the time that friends had come to the house who knew nothing of the matter but they too sometimes caught a glimpse of the ghost of the hanged man and vowed never to return to the haunted house.

When Miss C. Jones, who now lives near Wrexham, was young, her family home was at Birkenhead. She told me in

November 1975, that her late father, 'a good living and greatly respected man' was always very methodical. In his later years he had been warned of a heart condition and although he had retired from business, he continued to live an active life of service to others. Every Saturday, with unfailing regularity at five o'clock in the afternoon, before the family had tea, he used to wind the wall-clock and often he would remark, 'the old clock won't go when I am gone.' He died peacefully in his sleep at Christmas 1931 at the age of seventy-one and the wall-clock stopped at the same time. All attempts to get it working again met with complete and utter failure. 'I am now seventy-two,' Miss Jones told me, 'but I can recall it all as vividly as if it were yesterday.'

The area of Poulton Road is said to be haunted by a phantom nun who died at Poulton Hall while on her way to a nunnery. For several weeks in 1970 motorists and pedestrians reported seeing an elusive phantom figure that disappeared on being approached.

One motorist said that late one night he was returning from a visit to a friend in Higher Bebington, travelling along Poulton Road, when he encountered the mysterious figure. It was quite dark but he saw a figure ahead of him at the side of the road. He slowed down and noticed that the figure was that of a female, a girl who seemed to have long hair, and she was wearing a long, dark coat and seemed to be standing at the roadside alone. He thought this rather odd at such a time of night so he stopped to ask whether he could be of any assistance or if he could give her a lift.

As the car stopped, he leaned over the passenger seat and opened the car window; as he did so the girl slowly disappeared. There was no question of her moving away in any direction. She was standing there, absolutely motionless one minute and then she gradually became less and less solid until there was nothing to be seen of her. Understandably the motorist was somewhat shaken by the incident. Looking back on the matter he realized that he could not recall having seen the girl's face but he knew that it was a female figure. He has never discovered a logical explanation and only afterwards learned that other people have also reported seeing a mysterious female figure in the area, a figure that disappears when it is approached.

Blackburn, LANCASHIRE

A few miles out of Blackburn, on the road to Preston, stands noble Samlesbury Hall, a fine old manor house, half-timbered and exuding history. Here lived Grace Sowerbutts, reputedly a notorious witch who narrowly escaped the usual penalty for such activities although her colleagues were ignominiously put to death. Here too lived Sir John Southworth, Sheriff of Lancashire in 1562 and a bigoted Catholic in dangerous times. He suffered heavy fines and several terms of imprisonment before his death in 1595. It is from this period that the best-known ghost of Samlesbury belongs.

It seems that Sir John's favourite daughter, Dorothy, fell in love with the Hoghton heir of a neighbouring manor; the feeling was mutual and all would have been well had not the knight in question – and his family – been staunch Protestants; but still the lovers met in secret and eventually arranged to elope. Unbeknown to them, their plans were overheard by one of the girl's brothers who was determined never to allow his sister to so disgrace herself.

So the young man lay in hiding as the knight and two trusted friends met the girl and hurried away; then the zealous brother sprang from his place of concealment and swiftly slew the young knight and his two companions in front of the horrified Lady Dorothy. It is said that the three bodies were hurriedly buried under the chapel at Samlesbury Hall while the distraught girl was sent abroad where she was confined in a convent under strict surveillance, but her lover's name was forever on her lips and at last in an agony of mind and body, she died.

Years later three human skeletons were discovered near the outer walls of the Hall, by the chapel, where the lover and his two companions were said to have been buried; a fact that suggests there may be some foundation in the original tradition and in the story of the 'lady in white' who is said to walk through the gallery (giving access to the chapel) and along the corridors of the Hall on still summer evenings, uttering soft moaning sounds as though still searching for her lost lover. Other reported sightings tell of such a figure gliding through the Great Hall and also emerging into the grounds where she is met by a handsome knight and two companions. As the lovers embrace all the forms melt away and a death-like silence pervades the still night.

In 1972 a married couple visited the Hall without knowing the story of the White Lady of Samlesbury Hall. The wife described seeing the hurrying figure of a young girl, dressed in a long and elaborate white dress, a figure that was invisible to her husband. Indeed, dozens of the thousands of annual visitors to Samlesbury report seeing a pale figure of a girl in and around the house while various guests, RAF officers and staff at the Hall have all reported a woman in white who disappears in circumstances that rule out the figure being human. When my wife and I were there for several hours in March 1977 no less than four members of the staff told me independently that they had personal experience of the 'white lady' and they had no doubt whatever that the ghost still haunts the house although they do not publicize the fact. While Joyce was absorbed with the antiques regularly on sale in the Great Hall, I kept an eagle eye open for the 'White Lady' but if she was among the friendly people in the Great Hall and elsewhere that day, I didn't see her.

Following a spate of alleged sightings a few years ago, when witnesses were interviewed during the course of a BBC radio programme, a former Blackburn councillor wanted to organize a 'ghost-hunt' with apparatus that included infra-red cameras, but the trustees of the Hall refused to grant permission for such an undertaking.

Other stories associated with Samlesbury include the murder of a priest who was discovered concealed in a hide, one of several at the Hall. The resulting bloodstains lasted for more than a hundred years. There are even those who maintain that they have encountered the ghost of the powerful and possessive Sir John Southworth himself at this very haunted place.

Blackpool, LANCASHIRE

The Royal Pavilion Cinema was thought to be haunted late in 1971 when strange noises and mysterious lights were reported by the staff. Early in 1972 a seance was held at the cinema in an effort to throw some light on the bangs and raps and luminous phenomena that seemed to be concentrated on the back of the circle. An entity claiming responsibility purported to be the driver of a horse-drawn vehicle who knew the cinema well in the 1920s and a former doorman and an usherette were accurately described.

The communicator had apparently been trying to make contact and having done so felt free to depart; at all events no further disturbances were reported.

King John, according to tradition, visited nearby Staining Hall from Lancaster Castle. The old hall had its ghost that was reputed to haunt the vicinity of the ancient moat, a Scotsman who had been murdered there. For centuries his ghost was seen, a pathetic figure wandering about the place, seemingly forlorn and lost but as time passed his form was seen less frequently and then no more. Yet the spot where he was murdered continued to be haunted by the unmistakable and inexplicable sweet odour of thyme.

An old house in the Layton area known as Whinney Heys was the scene of a barbarous murder when the owner of the property was done to death one day on his return home from market. Thereafter, for a limited period, the house was haunted by scores of irritating and vexatious exhibitions of a ghostly presence and then, quite suddenly, the disturbances ceased.

In 1970 some boys at Arnold School, Blackpool, terrified themselves when they conducted investigations and experiments into the rumours that the school was haunted. Arnold School was founded in 1896 and has some 600 pupils, some of whom formed an Occult Society led by Peter Roscow. He and eight other boys had permission from the headmaster to spend the hours from midnight to dawn in the reputedly haunted cellars.

All was quiet until the boys set up a ouija board with letters and numbers and tried to contact the haunting entity. Very soon they were getting messages that purported to come from a woman who said she had been murdered in 1854 by a man named Mercer who had used an axe on her. When she was asked why she was haunting the school, the reply came through: 'For revenge'. When asked, revenge against whom, she replied, 'The law'. The communicating entity was then asked to make her presence felt or known in some tangible way and almost immediately all the boys present felt that the room became icy cold although in fact they were next door to the boiler room. Some of the boys then began to feel frightened and the seance was brought to a conclusion. After the Lord's Prayer had been recited the room seemed to become warmer.

Meanwhile, in another part of the school, another group of boys were holding another seance in an old classroom and they later claimed to have made contact with a dead sailor who said he had been hanged for murder.

As far as can be established none of the boys knew at the time they conducted the seances that according to legend two former occupants of the headmaster's house were hanged for a mass murder.

Bolton, GREATER MANCHESTER

Belmont Road was once a favourite haunt of highwaymen and now, it seems, it is haunted by the ghost of a highwayman or at least a man who was hanged as a highwayman. Such a man, by the name of Horrocks, frequently operated in this locality and once, having held up and robbed a coach, he was surprised by the sudden arrival of a solitary traveller and in his haste to get away from the scene of the crime he threw some choice and individual pieces of jewellery into a hollow there, marking the exact position for future recovery of the valuables. Before Horrocks had the opportunity to retrieve the booty, however, it was accidentally discovered by a young man named Grimshaw and he, instead of handing it over immediately to the authorities, kept it hidden on his person, waiting for the chance to turn it into money. Someone to whom he showed the jewellery talked and Grimshaw was apprehended and charged with highway robbery. His story of finding the incriminating articles was dismissed as a falsehood and he was found guilty and hanged at Preston in 1780 and it is the ghost of the unhappy Grimshaw that is still said to haunt the Belmont Road, a piece of rope still around his neck, his eyes starting from their sockets and constantly endeavouring to protest his innocence. Yet no words come from the gaping mouth and no sound is heard as he ambles about the road on dark nights, so different from the Belmont Road that he once knew.

Terrifying incidents at the Social Services Hostel in Radcliffe Road in the spring of 1974 resulted in the residents calling a local vicar to exorcise the house and the four families all claimed that the house was haunted by the figure of a man clutching a knife.

Other disturbances included inexplicable raps, taps and knockings, doors opening and closing by themselves, articles being moved and the sound of heavy footsteps walking up and down the stairways.

One mother, who had resided in the hostel for four months, said that it all began on Tuesday, 25 March, when everyone in the house was awakened by a banging noise shortly after they had all gone to bed. Although all the adults got up to see what was happening, they could discover nothing, except that when they were outside the house they could still hear the noise sounding as though it originated inside the house.

After that comparatively gentle beginning things quickly became worse. The four families ended up spending the night in one bedroom and one of them said afterwards, 'We were terrified . . . we heard footsteps, doors opening and closing and many other unaccountable things.' Twice Mrs Mandy Whirity said she saw the figure of a man clutching a black-handled knife, standing in the corner of her bedroom. Finally, on the Friday night, 29 March, they could stand it no longer and at one o'clock in the morning they ran half a mile to St Stephen's Church where they borrowed a Bible which they hoped would bring them peace.

The Rev. Neil Handley, vicar of St John the Evangelist Church at Top o' th' Moss, Breightmet, was asked to carry out a service of exorcism and he commented: 'It appears that they had been playing with a ouija board before these happenings occurred. They may have opened up some channel, but we don't know enough about these things at the moment. The families are certainly very frightened of something and it cannot be dismissed as rubbish.'

'It is a very unhappy house,' he went on, 'by the very nature of the place and one or two peculiar things have happened. The occupants may have built this up in their minds to a certain extent, but the fear was there.'

Mr Handley, explaining that there was no set service of exorcism, said he had used prayers from the church service book, asking for peace for the souls of the dead. He said prayers in each room of the house.

One of the mothers said they had been told that the place was known to be haunted but nobody really seemed to realize what they had gone through. A Director of Social Services for the area refused to take the matter seriously.

In September 1974 two young Bolton people claimed that they were terrified and driven out of Trevor Davies' 350-year-old cottage at Red Bridge by a ghost. Miss Lynn Egan said the figure they saw was visible for what seemed like half an hour just after midnight two nights running on the landing of the cottage. Lynn's boyfriend Trevor Davies was there with a friend of his. 'Trevor tried to hit the figure with a stick but it went straight through it,' she told the local newspaper. 'And the figure kept moaning in deep, echoing tones, asking for a diary.' Trevor Davies said the figure had first appeared at the bottom of his bed some four weeks previously. That morning he had found an old diary under the floorboards of the cottage. He had passed it over to the landlord who gave it to a museum. Lynn Egan seemed to think that the ghostly figure would continue to appear unless she could get the diary back. She said the cottage went icy cold after the disappearance of the figure which was dressed 'like a soldier, with a cloak and sword and boots . . . it was absolutely clear.'

A council house in Leverhulme Avenue, occupied by Mr and Mrs Ron Smith and their five children in 1968, so frightened 23-year-old Mrs Edna Smith that she dare not go upstairs by herself to put the children to bed; she slept with a light on all night, and said she wouldn't sleep alone in the house at night for anything.

Two sightings of the ghost and a run of bad luck convinced the Smiths that the place was haunted. Mrs Edna Smith recalled that it was in June that the first sighting had taken place. 'It was a woman I saw dressed in a long pink robe. I saw her as clearly as I can see you, but only for a few seconds and I can't remember now exactly what her face looked like . . . it didn't look evil, though.'

Her husband, Ronnie, laughed when she told him about the figure she had seen but in the first week of October he saw the ghost himself. 'It was in the middle of the night and we were sleeping downstairs because one of the children was ill. Suddenly Ronnie felt something touch his head. He opened his eyes and saw something standing between the cot and the bed. He can't describe exactly what he saw but he noticed at the same time a strange feeling in the room – sort of heavy. He tried to get up but found he couldn't move. Something seemed to be pressing down on his chest and he felt whatever it was somehow got right inside him – inside his head – and then it suddenly went away. He had to sit up and smoke a cigarette to get over the shock.'

Even casual visitors to the house have remarked upon the uncanny feeling in the house and the family pet, an alsatian, is often restless and uneasy, sometimes wandering about the house growling for no apparent reason. 'It's as if he can sense something in the house and can't settle,' explained Mrs Smith. The children, too, seemed to be conscious of a ghostly presence, although their parents did their best to keep the matter from them. 'The children were always very good at going to bed but now they just can't sleep,' their mother said in October 1968. 'I heard Neil, aged two, screaming in fear one night and he just wouldn't stop. He can't talk and tell us what he saw but there is a part of his bedroom where he refuses to go.'

Before the Smiths began to think that their house was haunted a visitor, staying with them for a time, complained that he was kept awake by knocking noises at night; but it was the incredible run of illness and bad luck that really worried the Smiths. 'We never had a day's illness before we came here,' Mrs Smith asserted. 'Now the doctor is never out of the house. All the children have been ill and my husband; it really is nerve-wracking.' The final straw came when the youngest child, Paul, less than a year old, fell from a bedroom window and suffered possible brain damage. 'I'm not saying the ghost pushed him out,' Mrs Smith said. 'But I do say this is an unlucky house and I just want to get out of it. We didn't believe in ghosts when we came here but now we have to . . .'

The modern Institute of Technology stands on the site of some old workshops, premises that had long harboured an unidentified ghost. It was thought that the demolition of these buildings would probably eliminate or erase the mysterious figure of a man that used to be seen in the vicinity, most often walking along Deane Road; but in 1970 a similar figure was seen standing on the lawn of the college. At first the figure was taken to be one of the caretakers but the following evening, at about the same time, an identical figure was encountered by a local resident. Mrs Dennis of George Street said he looked just like an ordinary man, tall, thin and middle-aged with darkish hair. When she spoke to him, the figure suddenly disappeared.

The local Labour Club in Wood Street is reputed to be haunted by a Victorian couple. They were seen in 1973 by the club doorman, Malcolm MacDonald, an ex-Army man who was alone in the premises at the time; indeed he had just locked the doors so it was quite impossible for any human being to have entered or left the club. He was looking round, making sure everything was in order when, as he said at the time: 'Over at a table by the door I clearly saw a couple, aged about thirty, holding hands. The man was clean shaven and wore a Victorian frock coat and fancy cravat. The woman was handsome and wore a long, dark-coloured dress. They had eyes for no one but each other. I didn't know what to think and I just stood and watched them for what must have been several minutes; then suddenly they seemed to evaporate into the air and the room was empty. I was petrified.'

The club occupies the Georgian house that was the birthplace in 1851 of William Lever, later Lord Leverhulme, whose ghost is reported to haunt a bungalow where he once lived.

Mr MacDonald was found about ten minutes after seeing the two ghosts by Mr Richard Brazier, the club steward, who said: 'Malcolm was as white as a sheet. He was really upset and he's not one for making things up.' Mrs Dorothy Brazier, the steward's wife, said she had never seen anything at the club but she had several times heard footsteps when the premises were completely deserted. Malcolm MacDonald said afterwards he had seen some grim scenes during active service, including men killed at his side, but he'd never been as frightened in his life as he was after this experience.

In August 1971 Mrs Ivy Bromiley, tenant of a council house in Kay Street, reported regularly encountering 'a thick grey mist' that came into the house almost every night and hung by her bed. At the same time she had the impression that something was pressing against her throat so firmly that she almost choked.

The ghost, nicknamed 'Charlie', became so frightening that a local clergyman was asked to bless the house. The ghost was thought to be that of a former occupant of the house who couldn't stand anyone else living in the house and was trying to drive the family out. 'It's like coming face to face with death,' Mrs Bromiley said. 'It terrifies me so that I can't move, can't speak and sometimes I lose consciousness. It is evil and it saps my strength.'

Her husband never saw anything, but Mrs Bromiley's father, Mr Frank Powell of Skagen Court, supported her testimony and claimed to have heard the front door of his daughter's house open and the sound of someone walking up the stairs and to have seen a really thick and choking mist; but on investigation the front door was found closed and there was nobody upstairs. Mr Powell said he had also noted that his daughter's health had considerably deteriorated since she had been at the house. When they had moved into the house Mrs Bromiley had been told that the place was haunted – cursed, in fact; but she had laughed at the idea at the time.

Raphael Street is periodically reputed to be haunted by the ghost of a man who hanged himself and the ghost is often particularly active when there are changes in the building, occupied in 1970 by the Hygenol Cleaning Supplies company.

In the 1930s a man named Harold Johnstone committed suicide in a small cottage that belonged to the factory owned by Edge's (a firm that made the famous Dolly Blue), hanging himself from the old wooden beams. Later the cottage, along with others, was converted into offices for the adjoining factory and on the site of the Johnstone cottage strange happenings were reported to take place. Initially inexplicable footsteps were reported by several of the staff and then some of them claimed to have been touched by a cold and clammy hand. Even a fierce dog, belonging to a security guard, refused to walk down the passage that was built over the piece of land once occupied by the Johnstone cottage and some of the staff also claimed to have seen the figure of a man, slightly built and going bald. Local people came to the conclusion that this particular ghost disliked change since they had noticed that it was always more active when alterations were made to the relevant part of the offices.

A security guard was so upset by the strange happenings – shapes and shadows he could not account for, footsteps when nobody was there and reports of cold touches by invisible hands – that he gave up his job.

One employee, Frances Gleaves, suddenly heard footsteps pass her and apparently walk through an iron fire door; another girl saw the figure of a man standing at her desk; and another member of the staff, who later left the firm, said she had also seen the figure and described it in some detail, corresponding with the other eye-witness. The owner of a nearby corner grocery shop, who had lived in Raphael Street for over twenty years, revealed that she had heard a lot of strange experiences from people who had worked in the haunted building and she firmly believed that there was something there that could not be explained.

The picturesque fifteenth-century half-timbered manor house known as Hall-i-th-Wood has a cyclic ghost that manifests itself each Christmas. The story lends some support to the theory that over the years a haunting runs down, for where once a phantom cavalier was seen to run up the wide staircase, now only the sounds of running footsteps are said to be heard occasionally between Christmas Day and Twelfth Night.

Historians have suggested that the original of the ghost may have been one of the Brownlow family who built the house, possibly returning in troubled times to retrieve some incriminating papers from an upper room. Since the footfalls always appear to mount the stairs and are never heard returning, it may be that the particular Brownlow whose ghost haunts the house met his death in one of the bedrooms and his last, frantic race up the stairway has, in some unknown way, become impregnated on the atmosphere of this lovely house – to re-appear each twelve months.

Ancient Smithills Hall in the district of Halliwell has several ghosts and a strange footprint, I was told when I was there in March 1977. Parts of the great house certainly date back to the days of King John and it is said that a house of the same name stood on the site as far back as AD 597.

The property once belonged to the Knights Templar; it passed to the Radclyffe family in the fifteenth century, to the Bartons early in the sixteenth century, to Joseph Byron in 1723 and to the Ainsworth family in 1801. Happily, in 1938, it was bought by the Corporation of Bolton and today this rambling edifice is partly a home for the elderly while the rest is open to the public.

The principal ghost is said to be that of George Marsh, a nonconformist minister who preached at nearby Deane in the sixteenth century; he was 'examined' by Sir Robert Barton in the Green Chamber because of his resistance to the Roman Catholic faith. He was left in no doubt that he was doomed unless he ceased to preach 'false doctrine'. But the Rev. George Marsh was passionately convinced that the Protestant view of the gospels was the correct one and he was so disgusted by his inquisition that, as he was being conducted down the spiral staircase to the Great Hall, he stamped his foot, declaring that he would never renounce his faith and praying aloud that the imprint of his foot would remain for ever as a reminder of his suffering and his divine beliefs.

Before long he was examined again at Lathorn House, the home of Lord Derby, and again he refused to renounce his views; a second summons to Lathorn brought the same result and Marsh was taken to Lancaster Castle and held there for several months. Under torture he steadfastly refused to betray any of his friends and he even preached and prayed and read passages from the Bible in a sufficiently loud voice to attract crowds of people who gathered at the prison walls to listen to him.

Marsh was transferred to Chester and interrogated by an ecclesiastical court but he remained unshaken in his convictions and he was sentenced to death. One spring morning in 1555, when he was in his fortieth year, he was taken out for execution. Even then he was given a last chance. An envelope was shown to him that contained a pardon if he would renounce his heretical teaching. Still he refused and, steadfast to the end, he was chained to a stake and burned alive. Today a plaque commemorates the place of his death and a memorial stone can be seen in Deane Churchyard and a ghostly footprint is still to be seen at Smithhills Hall.

In 1787 a visitor to the Hall described the footprint. 'I took notice of the mark, which is not unlike the shape of a human foot, except that it is rather longer than common: in the part where the sole is supposed to have rested, is a small dent, not much unlike as if a man stamped vehemently on the soft earth, and the weight of his body had principally borne on that part; the impression is of a dark brown or reddish hue and is most perceptible when washed with water, when it is plainly visible.' Arthur Mee stated that 'the footprint glowed red occasionally'.

One visitor enquired whether the stone bearing the mark

had ever been removed and was told that many years ago three young men of the house, in the absence of their parents, removed the stone and threw it into a gully behind the house. Their parents returned in the evening and when everyone had retired to bed 'strange and unusual' noises reverberated through the house. When the facts were disclosed the young men were sent to recover the stone. Some fragments had been broken on its removal and these were carefully replaced and the stone restored to its original position; thereafter the strange noises ceased.

The same writer was told the story of the apparition of a clergyman that has long been reputed to appear at Smithills. It seems that, late in 1732, a certain John Butterworth visited Smithills Hall one Saturday evening and slept in the Green Chamber. In the morning he was found in great distress and said that as he prepared for bed the previous night he had seen an apparition in the room, dressed like a minister, wearing a white robe, with a 'band affixed to his neck', and carrying a book in his hand. When Butterworth was in bed the form approached and stood by the bedside for a while and then disappeared. John Butterworth persisted in his story for the rest of his life.

A descendent of the Ainsworth family, Annabel Huth Jackson, in her book published in 1932, *A Victorian Childhood*, relates that for many years one room was preserved as it had been in the days of some distant forefathers. The chamber was The Dead Room and it was here that dead members of the family were laid out before burial. One wing was reputed to be haunted by the ghost of a cat and the rooms there were only used as spare bedrooms when necessary. One day, after some chaffing by visiting cousins sleeping in the 'haunted wing', several of them came down to breakfast next day with long scratches on their faces which no one could account for; they spoke with caution on the subject of the phantom cat thereafter!

Bootle, MERSEYSIDE

Bibby's Lane has a singular ghost: John Bibby himself riding in a four-in-hand with his head in his lap, and every New Year's Eve a phantom horse and rider are reputed to clatter down Peel Road, an apparition known as the 'Phantom Rider'. In Clare Road, in the house where once lived Mrs Mary Ferguson, a devout Roman Catholic who vowed she would return after death if her family did not provide a suitable headstone for her grave, the form of an old lady, descending the stairs but disappearing before she reaches the bottom, has been seen by successive residents, many of whom had no knowledge of the reputed ghost and whose descriptions of the figure they have seen correspond with that of the dead woman. Needless to say the body of Mrs Ferguson lies in a grave without a headstone.

Bosley, near Macclesfield, CHESHIRE

Five miles south of Macclesfield a gallows stood on Gun Hill until the 1880s, a grim reminder of the price of crime and of the murderer John Naden whose decomposing body was suspended there in chains after his execution in 1731.

One night, fortified with drink, Naden set upon and murdered the man he worked for, Robert Brough, apparently at the instigation and certainly with the connivance of Brough's wife. When the drunken Naden told her what he had done she at once set out and rifled the dead man's pockets to make it appear that he had been waylaid by thieves, but she failed to notice Naden's knife lying beside the body. The presence of this knife and Naden's inability to provide a watertight alibi was sufficient to secure a conviction.

Naden was duly executed outside the widow's house and afterwards his body was exhibited on Gun Hill. When the gibbet was eventually removed and the wood used for field stiles, people said the stiles were haunted by the ghost of John Naden, a dark and menacing figure that lurched drunkenly out of the darkness.

Bradshaw, near Bolton, GREATER MANCHESTER

On the Bolton to Burnley road out of Bolton, near Bradshaw Bridge, there is a tidy estate of some fifty modern semi-detached houses; the narrow road that dips down to the estate carries the sign 'Timberbottom', a name that holds a fascination for students of the macabre, the mysterious and the unexplained.

When he wrote his *Poltergeist Over England* (Country Life, 1945), the great ghost-hunter Harry Price stated:

> 'The case of Timberbottom Farm first attracted my attention in 1929, when accounts of the affair appeared in the press. This Timberbottom ghost stumped up and down stairs . . . and stumbled and knocked things over. The clatter of fire-irons was heard at night, but in the morning nothing appeared out of place. There were loud knockings in the passages, and shufflings would be heard behind closed doors, and on one occasion a woman said she felt "something" pass her, and go up the stairs . . . The owner of the property on which Timberbottom Farm is situated is Colonel Henry M. Hardcastle of Bradshaw Hall, Bolton, and in some correspondence that passed between us during November 1940 the Colonel told me some interesting things about the farm which has been in the possession of his family for generations.
>
> 'The poltergeist, I was informed, has infested the farm for the last 150 years. In addition to the manifestations I have recorded above, the poltergeist has a knack of opening and closing a certain chest of drawers in a room above the kitchen, in which many tapping sounds occur.

Sometimes the cat will follow the taps round the room. The "visitations" of the poltergeist are at long intervals: once nine and another time eleven years.

'Colonel Hardcastle related to me a remarkable story of two skulls – one male and one female – that used to be at the farm. Many years ago, during one of the periodic disturbances, his grandfather suggested, as a possible way of stopping the trouble, that the skulls should be buried in the churchyard. This was done, whereupon the most violent manifestations broke out all over the house. The Colonel's grandfather could only make a further suggestion that they should be dug up again. This was done and he put them on the family Bible, where they have remained ever since. The woman's skull, about six inches across, he had mounted in silver and placed on a stand. About nine years ago, Colonel Hardcastle accidentally damaged the mounting and took it, and the skull, to a Manchester silversmith to be repaired.

'That very day the most violent disturbances occurred at the farm. These continued incessantly until the skull was restored to its place alongside its male companion on the family Bible. Then all was quiet again for nine years, when a recrudescence of the trouble occurred in the autumn of 1940. The Colonel has asked me to investigate the case, and perhaps see what a medium can do. I have promised to help when the present War is over as Timberbottom Farm has great possibilities in the way of experimentation . . .'

Though Price had written in similar vein on the case in his *Search for Truth* (Collins, 1942), he unfortunately never did carry out any investigations at Timberbottom. It was, however, one of the first cases I explored when I came to write this book and one grey November day, in the company of my wife and our friends Freda and Steuart Kiernander, I found the sign 'Timberbottom' and after making a number of enquiries from local people, I discovered also the present whereabouts of the skulls, or rather their remains. Subsequently I unearthed about a dozen newspaper reports going back nearly forty years so perhaps we can look at the story in some kind of chronological order.

In 1939 the local *Journal and Guardian* stated: 'After eleven years' comparative quiet, the ghost of Timberbottom Farm, Bradshaw, has risen to activity again' and it went on to describe the experience of the tenants of the farm, Mr and Mrs John Heywood, on the night of Friday, 20 October.

Shortly before eleven o'clock that bright moonlit night, the Heywoods, having already retired to bed, were awakened by loud noises that seemed to come from below them, the downstairs quarters of the house. At first the noises merely sounded like doors being opened and then closed but these noises were repeated again and again and then they heard sounds like drawers being pulled out and, after a moment, closed again. Altogether it sounded like a search being carried out and the Heywoods looked at each other in some alarm as the sounds of heavy footsteps seemed to be coming up the stairs towards them. Then the sounds seemed to retreat down the stairs again; more noises, bangs and raps and rattlings were followed by the sound of footsteps again climbing the stairs, only to retreat yet again.

All this continued for nearly two hours until at length John Heywood and a lodger, Tom Lomas, who had also been awakened by the noises, armed themselves with stout cudgels and lighting their way with a torch, they set off downstairs to see what they could discover. As they reached the ground floor they heard the latch of the front door lift, followed by the sound of footsteps walking down the flagged path outside the house.

About a quarter of an hour later, after the weary men had established that nothing had been stolen or indeed was so much as out of place, and they had returned to their beds, the sounds recommenced and continued intermittently until about four o'clock in the morning when, tired out, the household eventually fell asleep. Before then the 'ghost' had ascended and descended the stairs several times making sounds that suggested 'a heavy-built man, wearing big boots'.

That weekend, Mr and Mrs Lomas, who had lodged, happily enough, at Timberbottom Farm for the past eight months, packed their things and left. Mrs Lomas seemed to be particularly affected and said she could never feel comfortable there after the experiences of that Friday night. She left the house 'looking frightened and ill'.

John Heywood, who was born at Timberbottom and whose family had lived at the seventeenth-century farm for nearly a hundred years, said he was impressed by the powerful 'visitation', adding, 'I should know; I've been brought up with it'. Usually the strange noises that were heard from time to time at the old house did not trouble either John or his wife but that night the noises had been so loud and so prolonged that he felt he had to investigate.

He and Tom Lomas had established that the noises centred on the living-room, but when they entered the room they found 'not the slightest sign of any upset'; doors and windows were all closed and secure and exactly as they had been left. Even the cat was undisturbed and they found her sitting on a chair by the fireside! They went into every room and found everything in order and nothing whatever to account for the tremendous noises that had so disturbed the household. 'It sounded as if somebody was lifting the doors off their hinges,' added Mrs Heywood. She had noticed two strange things as she had listened to the noises that awful night: the 'ghost' seemed to go into only one bedroom, a little unoccupied one; and on the last journey it had paused halfway up the stairs for about ten minutes.

At the time when she was interviewed by the local newspapers Mrs Heywood dismissed stories of groans, moaning and chain-rattling. She said there had never been that kind of manifestation. 'But it's as powerful as any strong man and it's there without a doubt,' she declared. Her husband agreed: 'It's been there since my grandfather's day and will remain when this place has been knocked down.' For John

Heywood knew that Timberbottom Farm was already condemned property and had it not been for the Second World War, it might well have already been demolished.

Once Timberbottom Farm was well known locally as Skull House Farm because of the two skulls that were kept there for many years but at the time of the 1939 disturbances the skulls had been moved to nearby Bradshaw Hall. It had long been thought that if anything happened to the skulls the ghost – or ghosts – would manifest. The newspaper took the trouble to ascertain that the skulls were 'in no way disturbed' on the relevant day, resting in their usual place on the Bradshaw Family Bible where they had stood for some seventy years.

The skulls, thought to be those of a male and a female, were formerly preserved at the farm where they were thought to 'maintain peace'. The skull that is thought to be that of a female was, even then, reported to be 'much mutilated' but the other is whole 'with the exception of the left side which is cut through as though by a blow from an axe'. Among the stories associated with the skulls is one to the effect that at one time they were buried in the churchyard of Bradshaw Chapel (demolished in 1940) and another time they were thrown into the river; but on both occasions, it is said, only when they were returned to Timberbottom Farm was there any respite in the house from 'frightful noises'.

About the year 1880, a local historian related a story of the skulls that he had obtained from an old woman who lived in the neighbourhood, a woman who claimed that the story had been handed down through generations of her family. As likely as not the story was embellished and altered over the years but it seems, according to this story, that Skull House Farm was for many generations tenanted by a family named Smith.

Indeed this tenancy is said to have gone back to the middle of the seventeenth century and one night about the year 1680 the family were away from the house which was left in the care of a manservant. He was alone in the house when a gang of mounted robbers came to the house and one of them tried to get in through an upper window of a room used for storing cheeses.

On realizing that the house was being attacked the faithful servant rushed about the house making as much noise as he could in the hope that the gang would think there were lots of people in the house and then, hearing the sound of breaking glass, he rushed into the upstairs cheese room just as one of the robbers was getting into the house, head first. The servant seized hold of a huge cheese knife that lay in the room and without further thought, chopped off the intruder's head, which fell into the room. When another member of the gang followed, he was treated in the same manner.

The headless bodies fell down into the yard below where they were picked up by the remaining robbers who had had enough of Timberbottom Farm and they made off, leaving it is said, a trail of blood that extended from the farm to Overs Houses Farm at Turton.

The skulls of the would-be robbers were kept at the farm until one night a lad named Davenport, more for devilment than anything else, took the skulls and threw them into Bradshaw Brook, at a point known as Lubby's Hole. Such however were the night-time disturbances at the farm that it was said no one had any sleep until the lad, having confessed to taking the skulls, showed where he had thrown them and they were recovered and restored to the farm, whereupon the manifestations abruptly ceased.

An early account of a noisy manifestation, allegedly caused by disturbing the skulls, is dated about 1850 when a new tenant discovered them and there was a lot of trouble until the skulls were reunited and respectively placed together on the mantelpiece of the farm.

During the 1860s the skulls were removed to Bradshaw Hall, the residence of the owners of Timberbottom Farm, and there it was intended they should be used as ornaments in a garden rockery but again there were such violent disturbances at the farm that they were taken back.

About the turn of the century, in a 'last attempt to curb the restless spirits', the skulls were taken to Bradshaw Hall and placed side by side on the Hardcastle Family Bible. It proved to be a wise move and all was well until one day towards the end of 1927. It had been noticed that one of the skulls was slowly disintegrating and that December day the skull was removed from the Bible and taken to Manchester for repair. Immediately the farm was plagued with noisy disturbances at night: hour after hour there were ceaseless footsteps and tappings and strange knockings. It was the same story, it seems, in 1939 when the other skull was removed from the Bible for a short time. Since then the skulls have never been separated although there were suggestions that they should be moved, under strict control, in 1964.

That year the Timberbottom Farm case was in the news again when a meeting of the local General Purpose Committee decided not to allow a Manchester 'student of psychic research' to attempt to call the ghost out of 'retirement' in order to study the results scientifically. It was reported at the time that members of the committee felt there might – just might – be a disturbance on the site of old Timberbottom Farm, demolished in 1962, and they didn't want to risk upsetting the inhabitants of the new houses built on the site of the haunted farm. By this time the skulls resided, on a Bible, in the Chetham Room at Turton Tower Museum.

Readers of the report were reminded that the last disturbances took place in 1939 when Colonel H. M. Hardcastle of Bradshaw Hall sent one of the skulls to be repaired (a statement that conflicts with press announcements made at the time). After the repaired skull was returned to its 'partner' all was quiet, went on the 1964 report, and the skulls were subsequently kept together until they were bequeathed to the museum in 1948, the year that Harry Price died.

A newspaper report at this time recounted the story of the skulls having belonged to two thieves who had been killed while attempting to rob the farm but, it was stated, 'it was eventually discovered that one of the skulls was female and the story was then changed and later versions say that the skulls are those of a farmer and his wife. The farmer is supposed to have murdered his wife and then committed suicide.'

Whatever the origin of the skulls, there is no disputing the fact that tenant after tenant for more than eighty years complained of mysterious footsteps on the stairs and of strange knockings and thumping noises whenever the skulls were moved or separated. Now the housing estate is all that remains to remind us of a story that suggests that some physical objects can promote and affect superphysical manifestations, and the skull fragments in their glass cases are silent witnesses to a mystery that must remain unsolved in the annals of psychical research. An enigmatic curiosity that is represented in the name of Timberbottom.

Bradshaw Hall itself was reputedly the scene of several ghostly happenings, including a ghost priest who haunted the place for many years. In 1930 a Colonel Hambridge was a guest at the Hall and during his first evening meal he remarked to his host on the fact that the table was only laid for two people whereas, apart from his host and himself, he had noticed another guest, clad in some long raiment, whom he had espied proceeding slowly and noiselessly along an upstairs passage in the direction of a hidden chamber which the owner had previously shown to the Colonel. Imagine his surprise when his host informed him that there were only two people then resident at the Hall and the Colonel had evidently seen the ghost of a priest that was reputed to haunt the upper storey of the Hall.

Earlier, when the Bradshaw family owned the Hall, there was a visit from a cavalier who was travelling incognito and disguised. After the visitor had departed it was discovered that Mary, the youngest daughter of the family, had been seduced by the gay cavalier and her brother vowed to have his vengeance should he ever meet the cavalier again. As fate would have it, the cavalier called at the house again, just as the brother was setting out on a journey. Recognizing the man who had dishonoured his sister he immediately challenged the fellow to a duel which took place at the front of the Hall. The encounter went badly for the cavalier, who was eventually struck to the ground and as his victor's sword point was within inches of his heart, the man exclaimed, 'Hold! Would you kill your King?' The young Bradshaw hesitated for a moment and replied, 'No! not yet,' and allowed the cavalier to recover himself. Meanwhile Mary Bradshaw, busy rocking the cradle that contained her baby, heard the noise of the fight and rushed to the upstairs window. Seeing what she thought was the death of her lover, she fell to the floor in a faint and smashed her skull on a protruding table foot. Thereafter, as long as Bradshaw Hall existed, occasionally the rocking of an empty cradle would be heard at midnight from an empty room and sometimes the ghost of the unhappy girl would be seen at the window of that particular room on bright moonlit nights.

When Bradshaw Hall was demolished some of the furniture was presented to Turton Tower, now housing Blackburn Museum, and when I examined the beautiful wooden cradle that had come from Bradshaw Hall, I was informed that sounds resembling the rocking of a cradle have been heard from the room where it now stands.

Historic Turton Tower has other ghosts, as the present wardens Mr and Mrs Walker, told me when I was there. Mrs Doris Walker has no doubt that the remnant of a ghost exists on the upper flight of stairs leading to the Chetham Room and more than once, when she has been alone in this part of the house, she has felt the touch of a crinoline dress against her legs. 'It's as though there is someone there who wants to keep an eye on something in the room so she watches who goes near,' said Mrs Walker.

A more spectacular ghostly appearance is the phantom coach and horses that several local people say they have seen drive across the moor on a route that was once an old Roman road. The coach drives through what is now a private house (once it was a barn that belonged to the Tower) and so arrives at the old entrance to Turton Tower, where it disappears.

Other possibly ghostly happenings include strange and unexplained noises at night-time: groans and thuds and odd creakings and an overwhelming atmosphere in certain parts of the lovely building; Mrs Doris Walker tells me that the Ashworth Room has 'a horrible feel' and she is always glad to get out of it. But there is no truth, I was told, in the story of a 'lady in black' who, according to one local author, 'appears to jump down an old garderobe shaft . . .'

On the other hand ghostly figures have been seen – and have disappeared – in the vicinity of Turton Tower. An old resident raised his hat to what he thought was a lady walking her dog; whereupon both the lady and the dog vanished before his eyes. And a hard-headed bus driver saw a man waiting for the bus near Turton Tower; he noticed that the man was wearing a light raincoat, grey trousers, brown shoes, a white cap and that he was holding a white stick. As the bus drew up the figure stepped towards the kerb edge and waited. The driver stopped the bus, pressed the 'open' button and as the doors slowly moved apart . . . found that the man had completely disappeared.

In the garden at the front of Turton Tower there is an enormous stone; once it was the lintel over the door of haunted Timberbottom Farm – if only it could talk . . .

Bramhall

Bramall Hall, a very fine example of timber-frame architecture, with parts dating from before 1590, has an unusual cyclic apparition, the little 'Red Rider' who is reputed to appear each New Year's Eve.

The original 'Red Rider' was a weary traveller who rode into the courtyard of the Hall one New Year's Eve in the

1630s, his red hood and cape blowing in the wintry wind. He was welcomed inside, rested, entertained before a roaring fire, given food and drink and provided with a room for the night. The following morning William Davenport, the owner of the Hall at the time, was found dead on the floor of the Hall and the unknown traveller had disappeared.

Vanished from the face of the earth he may have done, but there are still people living near the park and the Hall, now open as a museum, who say that a figure in red, his hood blowing in the breeze, rides again into the courtyard every New Year's Eve.

Bromley Cross, near Bolton, GREATER MANCHESTER

On the edge of Turton Moors, above Bolton, a seventeenth-century cavalier has been seen to materialize out of the walls of Old School Cottages in daylight.

A former occupant, Mrs Catherine Hormby, revealed in 1967 that when her daughter Rachel was about two years old she said she saw a man in the house wearing a 'great big hat' and later Mrs Hormby saw the same figure herself. She had just come out of the kitchen and as she entered the lounge she saw the figure of a man, dressed like a cavalier, standing in the corner of the room.

Soon after Mr and Mrs Richard Barlow moved into the cottage in 1965 they noticed that their three dogs sometimes acted strangely. For no apparent reason one would run round and round, barking away at something invisible to its owners, whimpering and snarling; she would be joined by another of the dogs and then by the third. On one occasion this animal, which had been asleep, suddenly awoke and snapped at something and then careered into a door in her anxiety to get away.

One summer afternoon Mr and Mrs Barlow were occupied in the outside barn that adjoins the cottage. Mr Barlow was busy converting the barn into kennels for the dogs when

Mrs Barlow heard the sound of soldiers marching past the cottage. She went outside with one of the dogs but the road in both directions and the moors beyond were completely deserted.

Later Mr Barlow heard the dogs barking and thought he heard someone outside. He caught the words 'peril' and 'menace' shouted in a man's voice but when he went out of the barn there was nothing to be seen.

During the Civil War Bolton was the first place in the kingdom to raise a militia force under the authority of Parliament and the history of the area relates that the town suffered more of the horrors of internecine strife and bloodshed than any other town in Lancashire. It is not unlikely that the barn at Bromley Cross may have once hidden a cavalier or been the scene of some long-forgotten skirmish.

Burnley, LANCASHIRE

The Eagles Crag at Cliviger Gorge is the traditional site of a witch's grave. Lord William Towneley buried his wife Lady Sybil there. Sybil was a dabbler in the Black Arts and it is said that she could turn herself into the shape of a white doe or a white cat. Before they were married Sybil rejected Lord William's advances and became deeper and deeper involved in occult practices. He consulted another witch who advised him to hunt the doe on All Hallow's Eve. With the help of a magical dog he trapped the white doe which then changed back to Sybil. She admitted that power was not everything and agreed to marry him and reject sorcery. But she did not completely revoke the Black Arts and since her death a ghostly doe, hound and huntsman have haunted the crag where she was brought to bay as darkness falls on Hallowe'en.

Towneley Hall now houses Burnley Borough Council's Art Gallery and Museums, a happy fate for a house that was associated with the rich and powerful Towneley family for more than five hundred years. One Richard de Towneley was a Sheriff of Lancashire as far back as Edward III; another Richard fought with Henry V at Agincourt; yet another Richard was knighted by Lord Stanley on the battlefield at Hutton and his son, John, was knighted in 1497 when serving in the English army that invaded Scotland. A later John Towneley was responsible for some of the beautiful wood carving still to be seen at the Hall but he was a Roman Catholic (like many of his forebears) and he suffered greatly for his faith, being imprisoned at Chester, York, Hull, Westminster, Broughton and Ely. When seventy-three years of age and blind, he was forced to remain within five miles of Towneley – so he built a fine doorway to the private chapel and restored earlier woodwork so beautifully that it is with us still.

Another John Towneley's tortured spirit will not leave the family home. Sir John (1473-1539) caused much hardship to local people by dispossessing them of their ancient rights of common land; he even had families thrown out of their homes on occasions and the houses destroyed, so that still more acres could be added to the Towneley estates. In later years he is said to have bitterly regretted his heartless acts and after his death his ghost was said to wander about the Hall and the estate, full of remorse for the dark deeds he had perpetuated. However, the present Curator at Towneley, Hubert R. Rigg, tells me 'there are no ghosts connected with the house itself' although there are 'stories connected with the Towneley family'. He quoted for me a local history published in 1801 describing the ghost of Sir John and its wanderings and also referred me to a later book, *Calderdale*, published in 1906, containing an account of the local people requesting the chaplain at the Hall to conduct a service in an attempt to lay the ghost. This is said to have been successful but there was a condition: the ghost would never appear while there was a green leaf in the neighbouring gully so the gully, or clough, was planted with evergreen holly trees and the ghost of Towneley troubled the Hall no more.

Bury, GREATER MANCHESTER

The Classic Cinema was reported to be haunted in July 1976, when a police tracker dog was 'terrorized' after a 'ghost-like figure had been seen in the foyer'. An extensive search of the premises and surroundings was unsuccessful but two hours later the police were recalled to the cinema when the shadowy figure was seen again. This time an alsatian dog was sent in but within minutes it came back, whimpering, with its fur standing on end. The incidents were blamed on the 'spirit' of a man who is said to have hanged himself in an upper room when the cinema was a theatre.

An assistant manageress, Mrs Irene O'Connell, had the surprise of her life when the ghost, nicknamed 'Old Sid', suddenly appeared during the middle of the screening of a film. 'I suddenly felt icy cold,' she said at the time, 'and then I saw the figure that seemed to be hovering about six feet above the stalls.' Her description of the ghost suggested an old-time actor in theatrical medieval clothes and a three-cornered hat; a description that corresponds with the figure reported by several people at different times and in different parts of the building but most frequently in the foyer when the cinema has been closed, late at night. In the days when the old premises was a live theatre the ghost of 'Old Sid' was often seen; if he is conscious of his surroundings he must find a great change for by 1976 most of the features showing at the Classic Cinema were of the x-certificate class.

Capesthorne, near Macclesfield, CHESHIRE

Near Macclesfield, seven miles south of Wilmslow and six and a half miles north of Congleton on the A34 stands the ninety-eight roomed house of Lt. Col. Sir Walter Bromley-Davenport, built in 1722 and haunted by a number of ghosts including a column of figures, a severed arm and a Lady in Grey.

The middle section of this vast house was destroyed by fire in 1861; all the unexplained happenings have been reported from the original parts of the towered and domed mansion.

Sir Walter himself, a former boxing champion, Member of Parliament (and Conservative whip) and a man not easily impressed or given to flights of imagination told my friend Dr George Owen: 'One night I saw a line of shadowy, spectre-like figures descending the steps into the family vault in my private chapel.' Another time he briefly glimpsed a grey form gliding along the corridor which leads from the drawing-room to the dining-room in the oldest part of the house. The figure's head was bowed and she wore long and voluminous grey skirts, yet she moved briskly and was soon out of sight.

Sir Walter's son, William, had a very frightening experience. One still, windless night, in 1958, when he was twenty-three, he was awakened by the sound of his bedroom window rattling near his head and when he opened his eyes he saw a disembodied arm 'reaching out from nowhere to rattle the window . . .' William Bromley-Davenport promptly got out of bed to look for a solution to the mystery but the arm disappeared as he approached it. He opened the securely fastened window and looked down into the courtyard, thirty feet below; there was no sign of anyone anywhere. Since that night the room has become known as 'the Room with the Severed Arm'.

Visitors to Capesthorne have also reported witnessing strange and unexplained forms and happenings. Sir Charles Taylor, MP, said he saw the ghostly form of a lady in grey hurry past the foot of one of the staircases in the west wing at about 10.30 at night as he was about to go to bed. His attention was attracted by the 'swishing' sound of her long skirts from the foot of the stairs behind him. He paused, looked down and saw the ghost floating along the corridor. He saw her for no more than a few seconds but the overall impression was of a lady in grey.

Another Member of Parliament spent a sleepless night in one of the bedrooms at Capesthorne where the door continually opened and closed of its own accord. He had previously slept undisturbed in the same room but on this particular night the door, no matter how many times he carefully closed it and even wedged it shut, repeatedly clicked open by itself and a moment later banged shut.

In 1968 Dr George Owen carried out an investigation at Capesthorne and he told me afterwards 'In my view there is no doubt that Capesthorne Hall is haunted, but the influence at work is mild and benign and quite possibly associated with former occupants.' Sir Walter took Dr Owen on a tour of the house, pointing out the various places that had been the scene of inexplicable happenings and when they arrived at the beautiful private chapel he said that he saw the phantom procession on the night of 3 September, the 250th anniversary of the building of the chapel. He went to the chapel to see that all was well for the ceremony and suddenly saw a line of eight or nine silent figures begin to descend the steps that lead into the side of the family vault. He called his wife, Lenette, who was in the library but by the time she arrived at the chapel, 'the clearly defined figures had evaporated'.

'I have no idea who the ghosts are,' Sir William told me when I was at Capesthorne in 1977. 'Everyone has their own theory. I just assume they are my ancestors.' Earlier he had told me that he did not really like talking about the ghosts any more. 'Whenever they have appeared we have had the spot blessed by the church and we think that they are all now laid to rest as we do not see them. To my family and myself, these ghosts have been very personal . . . I think we are dealing with something about which we know nothing but one day when we die very probably the whole matter, indeed the whole mystery, will be solved.'

Carnforth, LANCASHIRE

On Sunday, 7 October 1951, the then rector of Leek parish left the church just after noon and had walked only ten or fifteen yards along the tree-lined lane when, raising his eyes, he saw the figure of a man some seventy or eighty yards ahead of him. The man was dressed in modern style and was wearing a grey overcoat. At first the rector thought it must be a friend who had left the church ahead of him and was now waiting for him; looking at the ground as he walked on, the rector looked up fifteen or twenty seconds later and was astonished to find that the figure had completely disappeared. It seemed quite impossible for the figure to have reached the end of the lane at the pace he had been walking but the rector hurried to the end of the lane where it joined the fell road at a right angle. Yet on looking both ways, he could see no one.

From this junction it is possible to see two or three hundred yards in both directions and no one could possibly have walked out of sight in the short time it took the rector to walk the rest of the way along the lane after he had seen the figure. In a letter to me at the time the rector added that there were three field gates near the road junction but he would have heard had they been opened and in any case he could see the whole extent of the fields from the roadway. The figure was not that of a farmer or farm labourer.

When the rector reached his home he asked his friend whether he had seen anyone on the lane or roadway but his friend had walked along a field path between the church and the vicarage and had not used the lane or roadway. Such uncorroborated testimony may not be of great scientific value but the rector had no doubt that he saw the figure of a man near Leek vicarage that disappeared in circumstances that could not be explained in rational terms.

Charnock Richard, near Chorley, LANCASHIRE

Historic Park Hall has seen many changes and happy and unhappy times during the last seven hundred years: Sir Henry de Lea plotting against the Earl of Lancaster in the reign of Edward II; the Catholic de Hoghtons hiding priests on the run in Elizabethan times; monks meeting ladies in the secluded woods; great balls and secret trysts in secret passages – now it is an hotel and leisure centre with a banqueting hall, cabaret lounge, restaurant, several bars, a swimming pool and squash and tennis courts.

Legend has it that a ghost monk walks in the grounds, seeking his lost lady love – perhaps she is the mysterious White Lady that rises out of the middle of the lake. A former owner, Mr G. V. Few, his wife, their daughter and a manageress saw this arresting spectacle from an upstairs window. Mr Few hurried down to the lakeside and again saw the vision distinct and clear before it slowly faded. Twelve months later the same thing is said to have been repeated but I have no reports of any subsequent sightings although the present hotel manager, Mr T. J. Astbury, tells me that several of the staff have reported inexplicable footsteps, especially in the vicinity of the Banquet Hall.

Chester, CHESHIRE

The George and Dragon inn, situated in Liverpool Road, is a modern inn built on the site of a 1600-year-old Roman cemetery and it is reputed to be haunted by the measured tread of a Roman legionary on eternal sentry duty. Unexplained and unmistakable footsteps have sometimes been heard pacing the upper floor of the inn, from one end to the other, in the early hours of the morning. Twenty minutes later they have been heard coming back and apparently passing through solid brick walls in the process.

Part of the canal bank, not far from the old city wall, is haunted by a clammy, misty form that seems to rise from the canal and envelop passers-by on wintry nights. On 20 February 1959, Mr R. O. Roberts met this nightmarish vapour and was terrified.

He had been to see his wife who had just had a daughter at the City Hospital and he thought he would walk home. He was on the canal path, near Griffiths' old flour mill, when he first became aware of something strange in the nearby canal. He saw what appeared to be a pale grey figure rise slowly out of the water, constantly twisting and turning into a variety of weird shapes; sometimes transparent, sometimes opaque, it drifted over the surface of the water and rolled on to the path almost at his feet. He felt a sudden terror and tried to scream but no sound came and although he wanted to run, he found himself rooted to the spot, paralysed with fear.

The ghostly form advanced towards him and still he was powerless to move. With a sudden swirl it was all around him and he was completely enveloped in the cold, clammy, intangible vapour. He had never been so frightened in his life. Suddenly his sense of survival returned to him and he let out a piercing scream and raced away along the canal path and only came to a halt when he was halfway up George Street.

Mr Roberts says it was a sharp, clear night, with just a hint of a breeze but he has never risked walking along that stretch of the canal path on wintry evenings since that never-to-be forgotten experience.

Clayton-le-Moors, near Accrington, LANCASHIRE

Today Dunkenhalgh is an old English hotel in a rural setting, standing entirely in its own grounds of more than fifteen acres, but once it was a stately home where in turn lived the Rishtons, the Walmesleys, and the Petres. It is from the time of the Petres, at the beginning of the eighteenth century, that the 'Dunkenhalgh' or 'Dunkley Boggart' – the wraith of a young French girl – is supposed to date; a ghost that is said to walk each Christmas eve.

Lucette was a little French maid to Robert, the seventh Lord Petre and his girl wife Catherine who, in 1713, was left a widow when she was only sixteen, with a baby son. Lucette became a favourite governess and when a dashing young officer, a relative of the family, came to Dunkenhalgh one Christmas, he promptly fell in love with the sweet girl and together they walked through the winter countryside, their favourite spot being an old stone bridge near the old kitchen gardens and there Lucette and her handsome lover pledged undying love. Some versions of the story say that the young officer never had any intention of marrying a simple young governess; others say that he was delayed from returning to Dunkenhalgh; at all events when spring came Lucette's pregnancy was all too obvious and while the family were kind and considerate, the older servants made the poor girl's unhappy life a misery. Each night she prayed and prayed for her lover to come back to her but the days stretched into weeks and the weeks into months until Lucette could stand the loneliness, the cruel tongues, the unhappiness and her increasing size no longer and she decided to take her own life.

One summer night, during a storm, she ran out of Dunkenhalgh, through the woods and over the parapet of the bridge and into the swollen waters of the River Hyndburn that flows through the lower part of the grounds. Next day her body was found floating downstream among the reeds. She was carried back to the house and buried honourably by the Petre family but her unhappy ghost has been seen many times, usually in the vicinity of the old stone bridge where she knew such short-lived happiness.

A few weeks later her soldier lover returned to Dunkenhalgh, unaware of what had happened, but news of the affair had reached her family in France and, according to legend, one of her brothers avenged Lucette's death when he killed her lover in a duel. The ghost of Dunkenhalgh that has been seen wandering through the woods and standing sadly on the stone bridge is that of a bonny young woman – and she is most often seen on Christmas Eve.

So much for legend. Research into the history of the Hall and its families shows that the only young girl likely to have had a governess at the relevant time was Catherine, the last of the Walmesleys of Dunkenhalgh. The name ended when she married Lord Petre in 1712 but his son, born posthumously, perpetuated the name of the first Petre of Dunkenhalgh. Many of the family records are still extant, including lists of servants and their wages; in none of these is there any mention of a French maid or governess. Who then is the ghostly girl that haunts the Hall? In 1977 Mrs J. Burrill, the proprietress of Dunkenhalgh Hotel told me strange things still happen at the hotel occasionally.

Clitheroe, LANCASHIRE

Just outside Clitheroe, over Brungerley Bridge and situated on the north side of the River Ribble, stands Waddow Hall and here we encounter the legend of Peg o'Nell and a story of a curse and a water sprite.

More than a century ago one of the servants at Waddow Hall was a girl named Peg o'Nell and one night in the middle of winter a furious argument flared up between this servant and the mistress of the Hall. No one now knows the reason or cause of the quarrel or who was to blame but the outcome was that Peg was ordered to go out into the cold and dark night and draw some water from the nearby well. She left the house with the angry words of her mistress ringing in her ears: 'may she fall and break her neck in the process!'

Peg walked out of the house that was the only home she

knew, her eyes blinded by tears, and she disappeared from sight, clutching her pail and full of misery. She was never seen alive again.

Much later, when the wintry sun weakly bathed the Hall with its morning light, Peg's body was found down by the river. Her neck was broken. Some people thought she had slipped on the stepping stones that once crossed the river but others recalled a legend that an ancient water sprite needed an annual sacrifice still; others blamed the mistress of Waddow Hall and said there was a curse on the house.

Curiously enough, following her death, the ghost of Peg o'Nell was reported to haunt Waddow Hall, disturbing the night with footsteps, sobbing sounds and manifestations of a slight, shy little figure that fled and disappeared almost as soon as it was sighted. By day the whole household and the servants in particular would be disrupted by the sounds of a clattering pail and by numerous and curious accidents that were blamed on the ghostly Peg. For years the trouble continued and whenever an animal died or someone from the Hall met with an accident, it was said to be Peg o'Nell seeking revenge.

The old legend of a water sprite (that some people thought had been responsible for her death) returned to the area, changed to accommodate the servant girl and now it was said she demanded a life every seven years and to this end animals used to be sacrificed in the waters of the Ribble to placate the vengeful sprite and to avoid the necessity of a human victim. Sometimes, however, a human life was thought to be claimed; on one occasion a late traveller, scoffing at warnings, decided to take a short cut across the stepping stones on the sacrificial day and next morning his body was found downstream.

So the years passed and then one local farmer, who had suffered many misfortunes which he blamed on Peg o'Nell, took matters into his own hands and vented his anger on a stone effigy of the servant girl that had been erected near the well where she had been sent to fetch water on the day she died. Taking a mighty swing at the statue with his axe, the farmer beheaded it. Thereafter it was thought that Peg o'Nell's powers were considerably curtailed; she could no longer travel far and wide about the district and gradually reports of her vicious powers and her occasional appearances entirely ceased. But still the headless statue of Peg o'Nell leans forlornly against the fence surrounding the well that bears her name in the grounds of Waddow Hall, a silent reminder of a legend, a curse and a water sprite.

Waddow Hall is now owned by the Girl Guides Association (there is something like poetic justice in that!); it is private property and the public are not welcome. In January 1977 the Guider-in-Charge, Miss Moira E. Walker, told me that they consider 'the doubtful story of Peg o'Nell ... very exaggerated and mainly fictitious'; nevertheless it is part of Lancashire's folklore.

Colne, LANCASHIRE

Victorian Colne Hall, situated behind the Colne Co-operative complex in Albert Road, started life as a manor house – it had become a beer hall before the Co-op purchased the property. More recently, it has been taken over by a Norwegian curtaining firm and workers at the Princess of Norway were saying in October 1976 that they were seeing and hearing things they could not explain, similar happenings having been reported from the old building years ago.

A former caretaker, Mr Fred Pearson, had no doubt about the matter. 'The ghost is there sure enough,' he said. 'I worked there for twenty-seven years so I should know.' He recalled once meeting the figure of a little girl in the boiler room. 'She wore old-fashioned clothes and appeared suddenly, right beside me as I was stoking up the boiler. A minute later she had disappeared.'

Dogs, notoriously psychic and sensitive creatures, have acted strangely in the building on many occasions. Mr Pearson remembered an alsatian being strangely reluctant to go anywhere near some parts of the building, especially one stairway and one particular room and when the animal was forced to be there, it showed signs of terror and ran away from the place as soon as it could. Shortly afterwards a labrador behaved in exactly the same fashion in exactly the same part of Colne Hall.

Many times, in Fred Pearson's personal experience, doors opened and closed by themselves, footsteps sounded about the building that were caused by no human being, and more than once, although he knew he was alone in the building, he had the distinct impression that he was not alone.

Reports in 1976 tended to confirm most of these experiences. During September and October strange footsteps were heard that could not have been the result of a living person; a woman claimed to see a figure, possibly that of a child; and various doors opened and closed by themselves. The phantom form walked past the worker who was not at first frightened but the experience rather upset some of the other women, not a few of whom said they had heard the ghost walking about the building.

A couple of miles outside Colne on the A6068 is Laneshaw Bridge, a village that saw a celebrated eighteenth-century murder. On Sunday, 19 July 1789, a local girl, comely and popular Hannah Corbridge, left her father's house with her lover Christopher Hartley, a treacherous youth of nineteen, by whom she was already 'big with child' (as the parish register puts it). She was never seen alive again but a week later her body was found in a ditch. She had been poisoned and her throat was cut with such force that her head was only attached to her body by two strands of tissue. It seems that Hartley poisoned her but when the poison didn't act quickly he cut her throat and threw the body into an oaken trunk at his home in neighbouring Barnside before burying it in a ditch not far from Barnside Hall.

Bonny Hannah was a familiar sight when she had been alive, walking over the springy moors and through the lush dells, and she always had a friendly smile and a kind word for everyone. When she had been missing for a few days, some of the villagers went to see a wise man and he told them exactly where she would be found.

But it is not only the ghost of poor Hannah who haunts the area of her untimely death. There is, or was, the miracle of blood oozing from a stone that merits inclusion here. Years after the murder, Barnside Hall was pulled down and some of the stones were removed to repair Laneshaw Bridge. Before long stories began to circulate that drops of blood could sometimes be seen oozing out of some of the stones that once formed part of Barnside Hall. Certainly crowds of people, from near and far, visited Laneshaw Bridge and many were satisfied that they witnessed a supernatural event, for there was no doubt that sometimes there was a reddish appearance to some of the stones. The superstitious became convinced that after committing the dreadful and bloody murder, Hartley had wiped his hands against the stones and the life-blood of poor, sweet Hannah seeped into the stones and was sometimes washed out by the pure waters that tumbled under Laneshaw Bridge. For many years after the murder the ghost of Hannah was reported to be seen, especially on Sunday evenings, in various places in the neighbourhood but most frequently in the vicinity of Earl Hall, close to Barnside Hall, near where the murder took place. At one time her ghost appeared so regularly that the farmer and his family became alarmed and sent for a priest to 'lay' her but Hannah had learned her lesson the hard way: she trusted no one and the priest was hard put to get rid of the sorrowing Hannah; indeed there are those who say that she still walks occasionally among the moors and the fells that she loved.

Crewe, CHESHIRE

The old Victorian theatre, in Heath Street, has at least three ghosts. The theatre stands on the site of a Roman Catholic church and graveyard and it began life in the adopted church building reconstructed as The Lyceum in 1887, a building that was destroyed by fire in 1910. The following year a New Theatre was built and so titled it continued to serve the neighbourhood with plays and shows through the First World War and into the early part of the Second, when it was closed for a time. It was revived briefly in 1946 and saw striptease, wrestling, bingo and amateur talent contests; now, happily, it is going strong with a high standard of repertory productions. And through much of its long history there have been periodical reports of sightings of each of the three ghosts: the wandering spirit of a conscience-stricken monk; the sad apparition of a ballet dancer who hanged herself in a dressing-room; and an old forgotten actor who haunts the area of the stage-door. In 1869 the ghosts were especially active and troublesome and a service of exorcism was held in the theatre but still, I am told, visiting actors and actresses and the occasional patron or member of the backstage staff sometimes encounter one or other of these three phantom forms.

Croston, LANCASHIRE

The Gradwells of Croston inherited, in 1571, a house haunted by an apparition known as the Sarscowe Lady, a shy ghost that was rarely seen and often heard. The legend, handed down through the centuries, tells of a girl from nearby Sarscowe Farm who fell in love with one of the resident chaplains maintained at Gradwells, for whom a hide was constructed under the great hearth of the house and an underground escape route prepared that led to Croston Church. The love-lorn priest became ill and when he died the grief-stricken maiden, in her despair, jumped or fell down the deep well at the back of the house but some part of her always remained attached to the house and grounds. Over the years there are reports of encounters with a slim, white, female form and many more of strange noises, movement of furniture, the rustle of feminine clothes and light footsteps on the old staircase. Today Mr Martin H. Kevill's fine collection of horse-drawn vehicles is set out in the grounds of Gradwell's farm and he tells me that when he arrived there, twenty-five years ago, he was informed that the place was haunted and many people had seen the apparition. Soon after his arrival he heard, five times in one week, distinct footsteps on the upstairs landing. On the Sunday of that week he removed a stone cross from the orchard (commemorating a chaplain at Gradwells named Winckley) since it had been suggested that it would look nicer in the garden. Four hours later a bus stopped at the end of the drive and the bus driver refused to proceed because, he said, he was sure he had run over a woman – and everyone said it was the Sarscowe Lady walking again. Yet, after that farewell appearance, the resiting of the priest's cross seems to have placated the ghost that walked for centuries; although Martin Kevill told me when I was there in March 1977, that some curious activity has been reported from the barn next to the house. This building was once a church and showers of stones, the sound of strenuous breathing and other apparently inexplicable noises were reported by an investigator from a Preston society interested in psychical research in 1975.

Disley, CHESHIRE

Proud Lyme Park stands eight hundred feet above sea level on the borders of Cheshire, Lancashire and Derbyshire – the name Lyme is derived from the Latin 'limes' for border – and, now a National Trust property containing period furniture and tapestries, Grinling Gibbons carvings and a secret panel, it seems to brood silently on its past – it certainly did when I was there one autumn day in 1976.

Glanville Squiers, that mine of information on secret hiding places, told me about the fascinating one at Lyme: an actual picture that swings out of its frame. The picture, a full-length portrait representing the Black Prince that came from St James's Palace, hangs on the north wall of the hall. It stands out from its companion portraits for it is set in a massive frame in the centre of the end wall and this frame was originally the frame of a door. During alterations in the early eighteenth century the level of this large and lofty apartment was dropped some eight or nine feet and the architect covered the gap on that side with this large picture. It has hinges on one side, and a cord and pulley at the top to assist in drawing it back to its frame after it has been swung out. The floor of the drawing-room on the other side of the wall is level with the bottom of the picture and this room is lined with old panelling in which there is a well-concealed double door which opens on the back of the picture. It might be thought that there was a secret entrance here at an early date but I am told that careful examination reveals that the door is a clever copy of the original panelling. The presence of the secret door is therefore puzzling although on special occasions it is possible for the whole arrangement to be thrown open, giving a pleasing effect from both rooms. Glanville Squiers told me that he had examined a genuine hiding-place in an old room on the top floor of Lyme Park, known as the Knight's Chamber, and there the floorboards of a closet on the right of the fireplace can be removed to reveal an entrance to two secret compartments, one behind a chimney being eleven feet long while the other is fourteen feet square and occupies the whole of the space under the flooring of the chamber.

The ghosts of Lyme Park are said to comprise a ghostly

funeral cortège. The 'House of Lyme' is thought to have its origin in the person of Sir Piers Legh, who in 1388 married Margaret, daughter and heiress of Sir Thomas Danyers, and he founded the family of Legh of Lyme. Sir Thomas Danyers had been granted the land, called Lyme Hanly, by the King in reward for rescuing the Black Prince's standard at Caen. The house, Lyme Park, was built by Sir Piers VII (1513-1590) but it is with Sir Piers (or Peter) II that the ghost story is associated. History records that he fought at Agincourt (1415) and it seems that he had only recently married the young and beautiful Lady Joan. Sir Piers fought bravely beside the King and when the French forces seemed about to overwhelm the English archers and capture the King, it was largely through Sir Piers's efforts that the enemy was driven back, saving the King from capture or possible death. But this was at the expense of his own life, for Sir Piers received multiple wounds and would not permit any attention to be paid to his injuries until all danger to the King was past. Then, it is said, he died of his wounds after the battle. History says he lived until 1422 and died of wounds received at Meaux but at all events his body was brought to England and the brokenhearted Lady Joan watched the solemn, silent and slow funeral cortège bring home the body of her husband-knight.

She never recovered the carefree happiness that she had once known and it was not many weeks before her body was found beside the River Bollin. Without Sir Piers she had no reason or wish to live. He had been buried at the top of a hill which was afterwards known as 'Knight's Low' or 'Knight's Sorrow' while the Lady Joan was buried where her body was found in a place afterwards called 'Ladies Grove' and ever since, when the wind howls across the moors and the clouds hide the full moon, the funeral cortège of Sir Piers Legh can sometimes be seen ascending the Knight's Low, carrying the corpse to burial, while following it there is a lady, dressed completely in white – contrasting sharply with the rest of the procession; it is the ghost of Lady Joan and the sound of her sobs and uncontrollable weeping is, it has been said, clearly heard above the moaning of the wind. And still the phantom funeral winds its weary way up the hill – and disappears.

The Conservative Club in Disley is supposed to be haunted by the ghost of a man in a light suit: a grey, bowed and elderly man who answers the description of an old member of the club who died from a heart attack in a chair by the side of the bar. The chair was moved to the cellar and afterwards the man's ghost was seen occupying the chair in which he had died. Other disturbances have included footsteps in the upstairs bar and a curious, difficult-to-describe feeling of being followed and watched.

There is a haunted spot of ground nearby, between Disley and Whaley, but no one seems to know what shape or form the haunting takes. It was on 16 July 1823 that businessman William Wood was returning home to Eyam from Manchester. Not far from Whaley Bridge he was stopped by three highway robbers and, when he refused their demands for whatever cash and valuables he had on his person, he was savagely attacked, beaten to the ground and his skull smashed with a piece of rock that one of the men wielded. Taking all the money and valuables, they left the body, its head battered and bloody and forced deep into the ground by the severity of the assailant's attack.

The authorities soon apprehended one of the culprits, Joseph Dale, and he was hanged at Chester on 21 April 1824, but the other two escaped, although one is said to have later confessed to his complicity on his death-bed. Meanwhile the remains of William Wood were buried and fifty years later a stone memorial was erected to his memory on the spot where he was murdered. By that time the place had become a haunted spot where few would venture after darkness had fallen and for years the hollow made by the murdered man's head seemed to refuse all efforts to fill it in and no grass grew in that little hollow. In 1859 Alfred Fryer filled in the hole with stones but next day they were found scattered in all directions and the depression was as empty as it had been ever since the murder, thirty-six years before. Another man, John Fox, rammed the hole full of earth and stones and stamped turf over it but next day the hole was empty again.

Droylsden, GREATER MANCHESTER

Picturesque and quaint Clayton Hall – a moated, half-timbered property with a bell turret – is reputed to harbour the 'Clayton Hall Boggart', an all-too-frequent visitor of the poltergeist variety that disturbed inhabitants by making noises that sounded like rattling chains, heavy weights being dragged across the floor, bells and heavy thumping sounds.

The boggart (again in common with poltergeists) also enjoyed interfering with beds and bedclothes and seemed to delight in preventing people, especially young people, from getting rest and sleep. Eventually a local clergyman is said to have brought quiet to Clayton Hall by pronouncing terms for the continuation of the disturbances:

> Whilst ivy climbs and holly is green
> Clayton Hall Boggart shall no more be seen.

As far as I can ascertain, the boggart never was seen. In any case, it is most unusual for poltergeist activity to be brought to a stop by such methods – perhaps, like a clergyman I know who tried to exorcise a poltergeist, it attached itself to the clergyman and went away with him!

Eccles, GREATER MANCHESTER

Nearly fifty years ago strange happenings were reported from a house in Liverpool Road, reports that caused something of a sensation locally and further afield. After living at the house for two years the Lees family disclosed that they had all seen a dark figure, dressed like a priest, walking down the stairs and disappearing through a solid wall. Strange noises had disturbed their sleep from time to time, noises that continued for several hours at a time. Occasionally, when they were awakened by the noises, they found that their beds had been moved into different positions in their bedroom. They tried changing bedrooms but it made no difference. The family were at a loss to identify the apparition although neighbours and local people seemed to think that it might be the ghost of a Father Sharrock who had died in the house forty years earlier. After several unsuccessful attempts at exorcism, an extended service, including the sprinkling of holy water, the blessing of every room in the house and prayers for the repose of the dead priest's soul, seemed to have the desired effect.

Eccleston, near Chorley, LANCASHIRE

Heskin Hall is now once again a private residence, the home of Major and Mrs J. M. Glynn; in recent years it has been a School of Management under Lancashire County Council but its weathered stone gateposts and much of the existing building dates back to the reign of Elizabeth I and it must have seen stirring times during the Civil War of 1642-9 when this part of Lancashire was a Royalist stronghold and suffered vigorous and often brutal treatment from Cromwellian forces.

Many of the successive families that occupied Heskin Hall were Roman Catholics and the ghostly White Lady of Heskin is reputed to be a young woman who was hanged by a cowardly priest to save his own skin. Having been discovered in his 'priests' hiding place' by a Colonel Rigby, the district henchman, the priest immediately denied his faith. To prove his 'strong Protestant faith' Rigby demanded that the priest personally put to death by hanging the young Catholic daughter of the owner of the Hall, a girl of sixteen. This the priest did, from a beam still at the Hall and situated now at the top of the fire escape. Older villagers can recall being told by their parents, when they went to the Hall, to be sure to 'touch the hanging beam' for luck. The girl's ghost is reputed to haunt the house and more than one visitor to Heskin has been said to have departed hastily after a midnight visit from the ghost in the Scarlet Room which, although centrally heated, some people find icy cold.

In February 1977 Mr C. W. Cunliffe, the Head of the Lancashire School of Management Short Court Unit, told me that some versions of the haunting have the figure of the young girl being pursued by the priest in the bedroom nearest to the scene of the crime; the phantom forms at length disappear through the wall close to the location of the beam.

The ghost – or a ghost – has also been seen in the modernized kitchen but perhaps she finds it difficult to completely materialize in such a prosaic atmosphere for there she is seen only as a luminous presence; on the other hand a visitor to the Hall, who was alone in the house at the time, claims to have encountered a young lady who appeared to be so real that he spoke to her – no staff were on duty that night and the Warden was on holiday.

A large chest used to stand at the foot of the grand staircase at Heskin Hall and Major J. M. Glynn, whose wife was formerly Lady Lilford to whom the ownership of the Hall passed, has repeatedly told of often seeing the figure of a young lady standing beside the chest. After the chest was sold he never saw the figure again; and then he learned that there was a story connected with the old chest about a young Scottish bride who playfully hid from her husband in the chest but the lid locked as it closed and only much later, long after all life had left the lovely girl, was her body found by her distraught husband. Similar stories are told about several houses, including Marwell Hall and Bramshill, both in Hampshire, a story that has become known as 'The Mistletoe Bough Chest'.

Egerton, near Bolton, GREATER MANCHESTER

In 1953 Egerton Hall had been a home for blind women for twelve years and by the time they moved out, in the September of that year, most of the staff and the fourteen residents had become accustomed to the soft, silky, shuffling sound that told them that the ghostly Victorian lady was making her rounds.

The ghost was rarely seen but she often knocked on doors which would be opened immediately to reveal no one there; her strange, dance-like footsteps were heard time and time again on the doormats outside bedrooms and in the deserted corridors; then sometimes, if one was very quick, they might be in time to hear a soft tread dying away in the distance.

Twice the figure of a Victorian lady was reported floating across the country lanes of Egerton and into a house and each time a person in the house that was visited died.

Mrs Florence Wickham, the matron, told me at the time that the matter could not be put down to imagination: not only had the unexplained figure of a Victorian lady been seen in the hall – by a cleaner who watched the figure walk up the main stairway and followed only to find that there was no one there – but she blamed the shuffling, half-dancing footsteps that she had heard many times for wearing a hole in the mat outside her bedroom door!

An electrical engineer, Ernest Chadderton, had no doubt about the 'reality' of the figure he saw twice near Egerton Hall. He told me in 1953: 'After having supper on Sunday night about four years ago an assistant named Meadows and I were returning to our work and had to pass through a small yard. On one side there was a plantation that stood about six feet above the level of the roadway; on the other side there was a mill roof, the water troughing being somewhere around three feet from the road, while ahead there was a shed, causing the road to narrow. As I reached this point I saw in my headlights the figure of a woman. She was standing against the apex of the roof which is practically at road level. The figure was so distinct that I slowed the car to let her cross the road but at the same time I realized that the figure was rather ill-clad for the time of year and the time of night; it was then 10.15 p.m. and very dark. When the figure began to move I knew there was something odd about it and throughout the crossing, and I watched it for nearly twenty yards, it never altered speed. When the figure was about three feet from the wall screening the plantation of trees, she rose into the air and disappeared.

'After I had proceeded to my workshop and stopped the car I asked Meadows whether he had seen anything when we passed through the mill yard. "Yes," he admitted. "I saw a woman in a long grey skirt and blouse with her hair in a bun at the back of her head.' I remarked that I had seen the same figure. My own impression was of a long grey skirt, greyish-white blouse high at the neck, long sleeves with lots of frills; the figure appeared to have a full bosom, high forehead, hair straight back and arranged in a bun at the back; the whole profile was very clear and I should say the figure was definitely Victorian.

'The second occasion that I saw the figure was about a year ago and this time I was alone. I had been delayed at work and again it was about 10.30 p.m. on a Sunday night in January. I decided to make sure that the garage was locked and was making my way round the road, shining my torch on the road edge to see the way. I eventually arrived at the garage and was just testing the lock when I caught a glimpse of the same figure, travelling in the same direction as previously and just disappearing into the plantation; the only difference on this occasion was that this time, possibly on account of the very dark night, the figure appeared to be fairly fluorescent but still the details were clear and exactly as before. The figure appeared to be about fifty years of age and five feet eight inches in height.

'The first time I saw the figure, when Meadows was with me, I experienced a feeling of cold and dampness; the second time I had the feeling of being frozen with cold but at the same time perspiring very freely.'

Mr Chadderton went on to tell me that later, when he was being shown various parts of Egerton Hall by the matron, Mrs Wickham, she happened to mention the ghost and he cautiously questioned her about what had been seen. Only when he realized that the figure corresponded exactly with the figure he had seen did he tell her about the experiences of Meadows and himself.

Later still, Ernest Chadderton informed me that Egerton Hall was situated about half a mile from the mill and in the same valley where he and Meadows saw the figure. He knew of no connection that there might be to account for the same figure being seen in the two places although he had recently learned that years ago a woman had been murdered in the valley but what she had looked like and whether she was connected with Egerton Hall he did not know. In view of the close proximity it must be likely that the woman was employed at the Hall or was associated with the nearby big house in some way.

Edgworth, GREATER MANCHESTER

The idea that the Toby Inn was haunted, following curious bumps and other noises at night-time, came to a head in 1975 when the licensee, Mr Jeff Maycock, revealed that he had a photograph that he thought might show a ghostly presence.

The photograph was taken by a regular customer of the inn and it is possible to distinguish the figure of a leering man behind the bar. The landlord said that when he first saw the picture he noticed nothing unusual but since then he had altered the bar and his wife was comparing how things were and how they had been when she pointed out the face.

Even before the strange affair of the photograph, Jeff

had noticed odd noises after the inn was closed and a number of customers claimed that they had seen inexplicable figures in and about the inn during opening hours, and while he was not totally convinced that the picture proved anything he thought it more than a little interesting that someone had suggested the photograph represented a former landlord who strangled himself after falling out of bed. Another possibility is that it could be a previous licensee who collapsed and died from a heart attack just a few feet away from where the figure is shown on the puzzling photograph.

Ellesmere Port, CHESHIRE

In Black Lion Lane in the Ellesmere Port suburb of Little Sutton there is a house that was once named 'Elvan'. It is a medium-sized pre-war residence and it used to be haunted – and perhaps still is – by the ghost of a man in a brown pin-stripe suit.

Mrs Olive Carson now lives at Chester but she lived at the haunted house when she was a child and she can still recall the strange, sad feeling. 'There was an atmosphere about the place, it was certainly an unlucky house for us,' she told me in January 1977. 'My father lost his job and took the top off his thumb and I very nearly lost my life. My right leg was amputated and my left leg was only just saved. One thing has always puzzled me: is there any connection between the fact that my accident happened very soon after I saw the man in the brown suit . . . ?'

Her father's accident happened early one morning as Olive was dressing and getting ready for school. She heard her mother making the fire downstairs. Suddenly, out of the corner of her eye, and almost as though he had stepped out of the wardrobe, she saw the figure of a man walking towards her with outstretched hands, his hair falling over his left eye. He was smiling and seemed to want to be friendly but Olive screamed.

Her mother came rushing up the stairs to see what was the matter and, between sobs, Olive told her what she had seen. But there was no man in the room. The whole house was searched and no one was found.

Soon after this disturbing experience Olive had her near-fatal accident. For a month her life 'hung by a thread' and she only survived by a miracle. When she eventually returned home her parents had decided to move from the house. Settling down in a brand new house was fun, Mrs Carson told me, but nothing could make her forget the memory of the figure she had seen and shivers of terror ran through her whenever she thought of the man in the brown pin-stripe suit, and she has always remembered every detail of his appearance.

One of her neighbours at 'Elvan' often used to visit the family after they moved and she told Olive's mother that she was tired of people moving into the house and then moving out again shortly afterwards. One day she brought some photographs with her. Olive came rushing home from school and glanced with child-like curiosity at the photographs lying on the table and saw, to her horror, the smiling face of the man in the brown pin-stripe suit, exactly as she had seen him in her room at 'Elvan', even to the dark hair falling down over the left eye.

Olive went white with surprise and an unknown fear and gasped: 'Mum – that's him – the man I saw in my bedroom.' Olive's mother had by this time forgotten all about the incident but suddenly she realized what her daughter was saying. She knew that the man in the photograph had hanged himself in the bedroom that Olive had occupied at 'Elvan'.

Some years later, quite by chance, Olive met a lady who told her a story so similar to her own experience that she felt compelled to ask the whereabouts of the house where it had happened. It was the same house. This lady, like Olive, had never previously seen a ghost and never saw another. This lady did say that she always felt uneasy in the house and she could never account for the fact that her little dog, who always slept at the bottom of her bed, would never enter that particular bedroom but stayed outside on the doormat, his hair bristling and obviously disturbed by something.

Farndon, CHESHIRE

The old stone Farndon Bridge, crossing the sacred River Dee that forms the boundary between England and Wales, has long been said to be haunted by two small white forms. Back in the realm of fact laced with legend, Prince Madoc of Wales is said to have appointed the Earl of Warren and Roger Mortimer as guardians of his two small sons, the heirs to his extensive and valuable lands. One night, as the Prince lay dying, they took the two innocent youngsters and threw them far into the flooding waters of the Dee from Farndon Bridge and so gained possession of the Prince's lands for themselves. Whether they prospered from this cold-blooded early fourteenth-century double murder is not recorded, but for many centuries the people of Farndon shunned the long stone bridge after midnight and some of those who ventured across talked of two white forms that haunted the stone buttresses while others said they heard the sounds of muffled screams and gurgling, like children being drowned, echoing from beneath the bridge on stormy nights.

Fleetwood, LANCASHIRE

Old Rossall Hall was reputed to be haunted. There was said to be an underground passage running from the gazebo at Rossall Hall to the shore through which contraband was transferred illegally during the eighteenth and nineteenth centuries. A fall of sand in the tunnel is said to have killed a certain Lady Fleetwood or Lady Hesketh and thereafter her ghost walked at the Hall. The difficulty for historians is in identifying this unfortunate lady, although a Jubilee

History, written in 1895, describes the then-current stories of her walks. The family sold Rossall Hall in 1844, by which time the ghost story was well established and the present school founded. Sightings of the ghostly lady of Rossall Hall are still occasionally reported.

Farnworth, GREATER MANCHESTER

When Blighty's Club was called The Monaco a phantom lady was repeatedly reported to haunt the establishment. The club is built on the site of an old graveyard and during the 1960s the unexplained figure of an elderly woman was seen many times by members of the staff at the club, especially in spring and autumn.

The last hours of daylight, in the late afternoon, when the place was being tidied and prepared for the evening, was always the favourite time for the ghost to appear. The phantom form seems to have been that of a former servant, for the figure was sometimes seen walking about the corridors but more often apparently polishing tables. Each time the figure was approached it disappeared.

In 1969 a shimmering white light was seen hovering near the stage and between the tables and several cleaners reported odd experiences: strange noises coming from empty rooms and lights found switched on or off in one of the corridors. Local people believe the ghost is that of a pleasant, dumpy and quiet cleaner who worked at the club for many years before she died.

Formby, MERSEYSIDE

Tower Grange is one of Lancashire's most interesting houses: architecturally it represents, in a fascinating and picturesque way, a dozen different periods. In 1563 it was described as an ancient building, 'old and ruinous', but at the beginning of the present century it was rescued from oblivion by an architect named Atkinson, who restored the property with old materials, imagination and real artistry. Today Derek Hanson is continuing the good work and he has built a beautiful garden cottage that some 'knowledgeable' builders dated as earlier than the house itself! One of the principal bedrooms, with a wonderful wish-bone ceiling, has long been regarded as haunted. The ghost is said to be a monk-like figure that appears to be dressed in a black habit but sightings of the ghost seem to be rare in the extreme.

In May 1977 my wife and I spent several hours at Tower Grange and Tower House (originally one property) in the delightful company of Mr and Mrs Derek Hanson at Tower Grange and Mr and Mrs Arthur Cheetham at Tower House. The Hansons have lived there for eleven years and have never seen or felt anything unusual, but they live in the more recent part of this remarkable house – built in 1903-8 – as opposed to the early part now occupied by Margaret and Arthur Cheetham, where portions date back to the thirteenth century and possibly earlier. In 1290 the property was known as Grange Farm and belonged to Whalley Abbey; earlier still, in 1220, the owner was the Abbot of Stainlawe and this ancient heritage provides a possible clue to the supposed ghost.

The Cheethams told us their dog 'Chips' was the first member of the household to sense the ghost. Suddenly the dog stopped short in the hall one day with his hair bristling and obviously aware of something invisible to his human companions. About eighteen months later exactly the same thing happened again and then, on Christmas Eve, 1976, Margaret Cheetham was touched by the ghost.

Her husband had just gone out and for a moment she thought he must have forgotten his keys or something and had returned for them but after she was bodily swung half-round by 'something' that bumped into her, she turned to ask Arthur what he had forgotten – let alone to look where he was going! – and she found no one there.

Several visitors to the Cheetham house have reported hearing noises that sounded like 'someone trying to get out' and some have said they have had the distinct impression of something 'not of this world' in this lovely old home. On at least one occasion, a workman who had never been to the house before and knew nothing of the reported ghost and ghostly happenings said he had no shadow of a doubt but that the place was haunted; another workman who had known the house for years always refused to go upstairs alone.

During Cromwellian times a priest is reputed to have hidden himself in the priest's hiding place in the passage, where a poem tells the story of the ghost. The priest is said to have been murdered in the hide where his body was eventually discovered; in the large hide, which I examined, I understand a male skeleton was found many years ago. Twice, at least, the 'monk's chest' that stands in the 'haunted passage' opposite the hide has been moved by unseen hands.

Mr Derek Hanson agreed with me that the connection of the house with the Abbey of Whalley might provide the necessary 'monkish' link but he rather inclines to the view that somewhere along the line a priest has been confused with a monk. He may well be right; the general description of a dark-clothed figure could equally be attributed to a monk or a priest.

Previous occupants of Tower Grange have included Mr and Mrs Blackshaw and their two daughters who said, in 1962, that they had never seen the ghost-monk and indeed, if he really was haunting the place, he must be 'the friendliest of spirits, for every room in the house has a very friendly atmosphere'.

The history of the house, as we have seen, provides a monastic link and the traditional history provides a link with a murdered priest, but it seems unlikely that we shall ever now know the reason or cause for the haunting – always providing a reason or a cause is necessary to produce a haunting.

The beach by Formby Hills has been reputed to be haunted since time immemorial by the fearsome 'Trash', a ghostly black hound whose appearance is echoed by legendary giant dogs all over the country. They are all huge, with luminous eyes, and prowl desolate places late at night. Trash, a local name, is derived from the noise the beast makes as it paces through the wet sand. In 1962, two staff reporters and a photographer from a local newspaper paid a Hallowe'en night visit to Formby Beach in search of the ghost animal.

Two of them heard and saw a 'huge, dark shape moving about in clear silhouette atop a nearby sand dune'. As they watched it 'took on the definite form of a dog'. They moved forward and the 'strangely compelling' shape began to move about in circles, much as a dog would. They hurriedly climbed the high sand dune but when they reached the top there was nothing to be seen, nor were there any footprints or any disturbance of the sand. They said in their report: 'It is impossible to describe exactly how we felt in print. Though it may easily have been a trick of the imagination, or perhaps even a stray dog, we are sincerely convinced that what we saw and heard was not of this world.'

Foulridge, near Colne, LANCASHIRE

Near the great reservoir that is known as Lake Burwain there is an early eighteenth-century farmhouse, called 'Hobstones'. 'Hob' was the old word for fairy and hobgoblins were mischievous elves or bogeymen; it is a fact that today there are many 'fairy rings' in the area and there are frequent stories of animals, especially dogs, showing signs of fear for no apparent reason hereabouts.

Once upon a time this locality was thought to be occupied by fairies and there are persistent stories of a very ancient burial place being situated somewhere in the area.

In 1959, strange happenings at Hobstones cottage revived these stories. The occupant at the time maintained that he was occupied on the outside toilet when the door opened and he saw a dwarfish figure that resembled a monk with a gnarled and twisted face, holding out a bleeding arm from which the hand had been cut off at the wrist.

The poor man was so startled, for this took place in broad daylight, that he stared, open-mouthed, at the mute and motionless figure for several minutes. Then the figure suddenly disappeared: one moment it was there, the next it had gone.

The days and weeks passed and the man and his wife had come to the conclusion that the curious experience must have been the result of some practical joke. Then the same figure appeared again, suddenly from nowhere, and positioned itself facing the surprised husband and wife. It stood and stared at them both for a moment and then moved towards them before it seemed to melt into invisibility when it was about an arm's length away.

After that the ghostly little monk with his ghastly wound began to appear frequently in the cottage and in the garden and at length it was arranged that a medium should visit the place, without knowing anything of what had happened. As soon as she arrived she registered an uneasy feeling and she said she had the distinct impression of a monastery and a tormented monk. She accurately described the figure seen by the residents and the upshot was that before long the cottage was empty. Later occupants have not, as far as I am aware, been troubled by the arresting and disturbing apparition of a dwarf monk with a mutilated arm.

Gawsworth, Macclesfield, CHESHIRE

Gawsworth Hall has several ghosts and the present occupant, Mr Raymond Richards, tells me that the beautiful sixteenth-century half-timbered manor house with a tilting ground formed by the Fitton family, has certainly been the scene of strange happenings but 'all ancient houses must have unaccountable occurrences which are difficult to explain. A dwelling cannot have occupied the same site for nine hundred years without acquiring some influences ...'

Gawsworth Hall is the capital house of the ancient Manor of Gawsworth and we are fortunate in knowing a good deal of the history of the people who lived there since medieval times. Here, through the ages, lived the Norman earls, the Stanhope family, the Earls of Macclesfield, the Earls of Harrington and the Roper-Richards family; each in turn being Lord of the Manor and Patron of the Living. And for more than three hundred years, from 1316 to 1662, Gawsworth was the home of the Fitton family, one of whom, the wayward Mary Fitton, may well have been the Dark Lady of Shakespeare's Sonnets, a lady whose ghost is reputed to walk in the beautiful courtyard and elsewhere. She is most likely the 'lady in ancient costume' whose ghost is still reported from time to time.

There is also the ghost of an eccentric eighteenth-century playwright and professional jester, Samuel 'Maggotty' Johnson, whose final jest seems to have been to become a ghost by being buried in unconsecrated ground, a spinney known locally as 'Maggotty Johnson's Wood'. He justifies this unusual choice of resting place in verses on his tombstone. His lion-headed fiddle (dated 1771) is preserved in the dining-room of Gawsworth Hall.

In February 1971 Monica Richards, who occupies a bedroom immediately below the Priest's Room, complained of the smell of incense that sometimes pervaded her room. Next to the Priest's Room there is an Oratory with an escape hatch leading to the cellars. In 1921 a macabre discovery was made following the removal of an old cupboard: a human skeleton. The bones were later interred in the churchyard. No one has ever been able to discover whose body was hidden there but surely no one could have wished for a more beautiful place to die.

The five-hundred-year-old mansion now known as the Old Rectory at Gawsworth is also said to have once been the home of Mary Fitton, the charming and promiscuous seventeen-year-old who so enjoyed herself when she was a member of the court of Queen Elizabeth I. The fifty-year-old Comptroller of the Queen's Household, Sir William Knollys, thought himself in love with her; so did William Herbert who found himself in Fleet Prison after giving her a baby and getting her sacked from the Court. Her passions led her and Sir Richard Leveson, an old friend of the family, to have an affair and some say he gave her two children; certainly she had a child by Captain William Polewhale before she eventually married him – and what of William Shakespeare, a close friend, it is said, of William Herbert; could he too have fallen for the gay and bright-eyed Mary – and made her immortal? Be that as it may, her ghost has long been said to walk on autumn evenings through the avenue of lime trees from the Old Hall to the Harrington Arms, a countryman's inn that stands on the site of a farmhouse or lodge that Mary must have known and perhaps even used as a trysting-place.

In 1964, the Old Rectory was purchased by a former Stockport alderman, Mr Idris W. Owen. He became interested in the possibility of encountering the ghost of the amorous Mary and he waited up no less than eight times in the room where she is reputed to appear, but with no success. 'Still,' he said in November that year, 'I've not given up hope of seeing her one day.' He was addressing a luncheon to celebrate the opening of the Abbey National Building Society's first Stockport office, attended by Sir Geoffrey Shakespeare, deputy chairman of the Society and a direct descendant of the Bard. He suggested that he might visit Mr Owen's home one day, adding dryly: 'The Dark Lady might put in an appearance for a Shakespeare...'

In March 1977, my wife and I met charming Raymond Richards and his delightful wife Monica and, over sherry in the beautiful ground-floor library, she told us of the ghosts and ghostly happenings at Gawsworth Hall and Gawsworth Old Rectory. We talked first of Mary Fitton and learned that the ghostly figure of a girl has been seen in the vicinity of the church as well as the Old Rectory, the Hall and the roads between. Once, a man who does odd jobs at the Hall was returning very late one night when he saw a cloaked female figure which at first he thought was Mrs Monica Richards. He saluted her but she gave no indication that she had seen him and carried on across the road and he had to brake very hard to avoid hitting her. When he had stopped he got out of his Land-Rover to find no sign of her anywhere; this was about 2 a.m. in the morning.

At one time there were serious attempts made to establish whether or not Mary Fitton was buried in Gawsworth Church and, before the ecclesiastical authorities stopped the investigations, a coffin was located bound with narrow leather straps decorated with a floral design: an identical design to that pictured in some portraits of this remarkable individual who deserves a ghost.

Monica Richards told us that the incense had been noticed in particular on three occasions and each time it seemed to precede the visit to the Hall of an archbishop. Once the archbishop commented as he entered the Hall on the thoughtfulness of the family to welcome him with incense; the family had been thinking that he must have brought it! Each time the overpowering but localized odour has been experienced by upwards of four people; on the last occasion, at the beginning of March 1977, it had lasted only about three minutes but on the previous two occasions it had lasted considerably longer.

When they had lived at the Old Rectory all sorts of things had happened: the sound of smashing glass, a woman's voice, various raps and bangs for which there seemed to be no logical explanation and once Mrs Monica Richards saw the form of a man with dark eyes and a little pointed beard. At that time her husband was busy with his book, *The Manor of Gawsworth*, and any visitors were directed to her, upstairs. The house is a fascinating place, full of history and interesting features and lots of people used to call and they were never turned away. It was after eight o'clock one evening when Mrs Richards came out of the upper room and saw a man standing at the bottom of the stairs, almost hidden in an alcove. At the time her immediate thought was that he had left it rather late to call and she was a little surprised that her husband had sent anyone up at that time. However, she felt that she obviously had to show the visitor her customary courtesy and she went down the stairs towards him. Looking back on the experience afterwards she realized that she didn't notice anything about the figure below the neck but his face has always remained very clear in her memory and she has always wanted to see him again. When she was almost up to the figure it seemed to retreat and at the same time she felt a sudden pain in her chest, almost like a dagger being plunged into her – by then the figure had disappeared.

At one time, when they were at the Old Rectory, a student priest was staying with them and after he had been there some time Mrs Richards chanced to comment that she hoped he liked his room and always slept well. Oddly enough, she was told, he had found that he could never sleep until two o'clock in the morning so he had got into the habit of studying until the clock struck two and then he went to bed and always slept without difficulty. It will be remembered that the odd job man who saw the ghost of a female (Mary Fitton?) found that the time was two o'clock in the morning.

Goosnargh, near Preston, LANCASHIRE

Tucked away at the end of a lane lies a charming seven hundred-year-old small manor house, built in the form of a cross, called Chingle Hall, the birthplace of John Wall, a Franciscan priest who was one of the last English Roman Catholic martyrs. Chingle Hall belonged to the Wall family in 1585 and John was born in 1620; he was executed at Worcester in 1679 and his head is said to have been conducted on a grand tour of the continent before being smuggled to Chingle Hall and buried in the grounds. Today Chingle Hall is more famous for its many ghosts and ghostly happenings.

Among the many fascinating features of this lovely old house there is the large and heavy 'Y' knocker on the massive and studded oak door, the only one of its kind in the country; an interesting signal window containing the original glass (used to indicate to the outlawed adherents of the Catholic faith that a secret Mass was being celebrated); the priests' hiding holes probably built by Nicholas Owen and a pre-Reformation 'praying-cross'.

Over the years many curious things have happened at Chingle. A rural dean witnessed the sudden and violent rattling of two pictures in the 'Haunted Room', situated immediately above the entrance porch, 'as though invisible hands had grasped them and banged them against the wall'. The present owner, Mrs Mayard Howarth, also witnessed this apparent phenomenon. A police Chief Superintendent and his wife, shortly after dinner at the Hall at the end of 1967, heard heavy thumps from above the sitting-room. A single 'thump' was followed by a distinct 'thud' and then everyone present heard the sound of heavy footsteps, as though someone was walking across the room above. But no one was upstairs at the time. A little later they heard the sounds of something heavy being dragged across the room and a rattling noise, as of a chain, followed by more footsteps . . . investigation proved abortive. Two hours later a series of similar noises were heard and again an immediate search revealed no explanation.

Mrs Proctor, who acted as one of the guides at the Hall, saw the cowled head of a monk during the summer of 1966 when she saw a face peering at her through the window: a pale face, hardly human, surrounded by a dark cowl. It vanished as suddenly as it had appeared and later Mrs Proctor thought she saw the same figure during a pageant held in the grounds of the Hall.

A Mr and Mrs Jepson were visiting the Hall and were in the downstairs room, where there is a hiding place, when Mr Jepson saw two figures, dressed like monks, seemingly in the act of praying. After a moment the figures seemed to melt into the wall. A little later, in the Priest's Room upstairs, Mrs Jepson saw the figure of a man with shoulder-length hair walk past the window – which is twelve feet from the ground. Another visitor, Mrs Evans, encountered the ghost monk just as she was entering the Hall through the outer door in November 1970; she described it as a 'green, diffuse figure' that walked towards her and they met in the porch. As she stopped the figure turned and walked back into the dining-room and closed the door behind it! It was here, in the delightful dining-room, in front of a roaring log fire, that Mrs Howarth entertained my wife and I to tea one afternoon in March 1977 and told us all about the strange happenings at the comfortable and happy home that has become known as 'one of the most haunted houses in Britain'.

Many visitors have felt the presence of invisible beings: a Mrs Walmeley received a violent push in the back while she was standing in the lounge and she was quite alone at the time. Mrs Moorby, a sceptic on psychic matters, had a distinct and very unpleasant impression that she was being watched in a bathroom; the feeling became so strong that although she saw nothing, she felt terrified, especially when the room became frightfully cold. At last she managed to open the door and run down the stairs and she has always remembered that the bathroom door slammed shut behind her by itself. Mrs Robinson heard footsteps ascend the stairs and witnessed three raps come from inside the priest's hole in apparent answer to a single knock on the wall above the aperture; then more footsteps were heard and a sudden knock on the front door, but no one was there. Mrs McKay was in the Priest's Room when she felt a wave of cold air sweep over her and she saw some flowers in the room move as though someone was twisting their stems; then a table-lamp shook and subsequently a picture. Mrs Rigby was having a cup of tea with Mrs Howarth in the lounge when an old wooden plaque (which I examined) shot off the fireplace and landed in the centre of the room. Mrs Howarth's brother William Strickland saw the figure of a priest walk through the gate and into the field and Miss Ann Strickland has heard unaccountable knockings, tappings, and footsteps on many occasions. Miss Janet Makinson heard footsteps from an empty room and when she went into the room found that it was freezing cold; she also witnessed doors opening by themselves.

Mrs Howarth has herself heard many noises that she has been forced to attribute to ghosts. Raps and taps on the walls and furniture, footsteps from the upstairs passage and the stairway, bangings that have never been explained; she has also witnessed the movement of objects, door latches lifting, doors opening and once, together with her late husband, she saw, in the room over the porch, a kind of illuminated form in a cloak. They both watched the form for about a quarter of an hour and then it gradually grew less and less distinct and finally faded away. Neither of them felt in the least afraid, only interested.

Following a February night in 1970 that he spent at Chingle Hall in the Priest's Room with a friend, the Rev. Peter Travis wrote in his absorbing work *In Search of the Supernatural* (Wolfe, 1975) that they had experienced door-opening, a groaning sound, a light switch twice turned off and the sound of a heavy crash.

In March 1970 Mrs McKay had another experience. She had been visiting Chingle Hall with her son and as they left the Hall that evening and walked towards their car, they chanced to look at the window of the room with a priest's hiding place and they saw a human form at the window, a white or light-grey robed figure. When Andrew McKay switched on the car headlights and lit up the window and the room inside the figure appeared to be dense and black. It was in this room that Joyce and I examined the priest's hole which has been left open for inspection. Michael Bingham, a young New Zealander who was staying at the Hall, told us that on one occasion, in the presence of a witness, noises like bricks being moved had been heard from the priest's hole and when he looked he had seen part of a hand that appeared to be moving one of the bricks. As he watched it the hand froze and then disappeared.

During his stay at Chingle Hall Michael not only succeeded in recording the sounds of footsteps and other apparently paranormal activity but he also used something like three-hundred-and-fifty yards of film trying to obtain a photographic record of the ghost that, he told us, walked practically every night, and on the last few feet, which he had taken by remote control, there is a short section showing a small hooded figure moving past the camera and then returning before it disappears.

Michael also told us that one night he was sitting in the dining-room when he became aware that hands were lightly but firmly around his throat; he saw nothing but for a few seconds he was all too aware of an invisible someone standing behind him and firmly gripping his throat – Michael, an old hand at the ghost-hunting after several months at Chingle Hall, was not even frightened. Mrs Howarth told us that on 17 January 1977, a friend from Hull was staying at the Hall. She was reading a book by the fire when she heard the door leading to the staircase open, and when she looked up she saw a monk in a brown habit, and she heard him sigh twice, then he disappeared. At 3.30 p.m. on 24 January 1977, the ghost was heard by two visitors and this time the footsteps were very loud and walked from the haunted room along the haunted corridor. Sometimes the sounds are so loud that Mrs Howarth thinks someone must have broken in and she gets help and searches the house from top to bottom but no trace of any human intruder is ever found. At other times the smell of burning and even actual smoke has caused Mrs Howarth to get the fire brigade; not only have they found no fire but their thermocouples have established that there was no heat source.

Well may James Wentworth Day say, in his book, *In Search of Ghosts* (Frederick Muller, 1969), 'Here, then, we have one of the best authenticated examples of a haunted house in England . . .' He may well be right, but Mrs Howarth and her sister live at peace with the ghosts. One day I hope to carry out a scientific investigation into the strange happenings at Chingle Hall.

The Hill Presbytery at Goosnargh has a ghost monk that may be a visitor from the days when Franciscans served the old mission that came here from Whitehill. A few years ago one of the priests at the Presbytery often talked about a brown-habited monk that haunted the present living-room (one of the oldest parts of the building), crossing the room silently and quite oblivious to anyone who happened to be in the room at the time. The figure was never seen anywhere else in 'The Hill' and it always followed the same track, almost as though it were a kind of photographic image re-running itself in some curious way.

Hale, Altrincham, GREATER MANCHESTER

Beneath some of the front gardens of a row of houses in Hermitage Road, Hale (just south of Altrincham) near the junction with Hale Road, there may lie hidden a hoard of medieval treasure; a store of valuables that are marked by the appearances of a ghostly monk.

The story seems to be a mixture of fact and legend but the 'Black Friar', as the ghost has been named, has reportedly been seen many times over the years and usually in the same locality.

In the days of Henry VIII, the Leycester family home, Hale Low, stood on the site of the present Hermitage Road and Hale Road junction. Nicholas Leycester owned the estate and lived at the house while his brother Peter was a friar at Birkenhead monastery and he not infrequently took charge of the spiritual needs of the faithful at nearby Bowdon church.

With the dissolution of the monasteries the Prior of Birkenhead entrusted his church plate, including a beautiful monstrance and a chalice set with jewels and precious stones, to Friar Peter who took them to his Hale family home and buried them for safety in the orchard of the house.

Legend takes over here and says that the treasure will only be found when 'a true Catholic Leycester is back at Hale'; then the ghost of Friar Peter, the 'Black Friar', will appear to point out the exact location of the hidden hoard. The Leycester family lived in Hale from about 1402 and their hall (in later years reduced to Hale Low Farm) was finally demolished to make way for the present houses. The sloping ground on which some of the houses are built probably marks the site of the moat of the old house.

Peter Leycester, the Black Friar, died during the reign of Elizabeth I and his ghost, the figure of a friar dressed in a black habit, his face a startling and contrasting white, has been seen many times over the years. A particularly detailed sighting was reported by Tom Perrins of Hale Barns Green in 1850 and more recently an identical figure has been reported somewhere between Halebarns and Hermitage Road (formerly Leycester Lane) and Hale Road (formerly Long Lane).

Hazel Grove, Stockport, GREATER MANCHESTER

A pet shop in London Road, Hazel Grove, was the scene of some very curious happenings in 1973 when Mrs Carol Payne decided to improve the back kitchen of the premises where, it is said, a man hanged himself earlier this century. Before the work was finished she twice saw a ghost and experienced many things which she was totally unable to explain.

Once she walked through the back door and stepped aside

to let someone else out and it was only when she was through the door herself that she realized what had happened. There was no one else to come out of the house. She looked everywhere but there was no longer any sign of the male figure that had passed her and anyway the shop assistant said no one had been in the shop for half an hour.

Another time Carol was alone in the kitchen looking out of the window when she saw the figure of a man materialize in the backyard and then disappear by walking through a wall. She just had time to notice a jacket and trousers but was unable to see the face of the figure. She immediately rushed into the front shop and told the assistant, who knew the premises since she had worked for the previous owners. She did not seem at all surprised and said it was known that a man hanged himself in the outhouse in the backyard a long time ago and his ghost was seen from time to time.

Sometimes, when nothing was visible to human beings in the backyard, the dogs would suddenly bark furiously as they did when a stranger was present. There seemed no good reason for the barking, certainly no stranger was in the vicinity and they soon quietened down but obviously they saw or sensed something that disturbed them.

Sometimes too the temperature in the kitchen was found to be several degrees lower than the rest of the shop although normally it was exactly the same or a little higher; and what could be the explanation for those two or three times when the lavatory flushed by itself?

For a time Carol and her husband and their three children treated the whole thing as a joke; they even nicknamed the invisible man 'Fred' but then Carol decided that the ghost didn't like being laughed at. She was in the kitchen one day, talking to a friend about the strange happenings and generally laughing about 'Fred' when suddenly two boxes lifted themselves from the top shelf, flew some distance across the room, and landed in the middle of the floor. Less pleasant still was the time that someone – or something – clutched Carol about the ribs. When she turned round the pressure ceased and no one was anywhere near her. Then there was the time that scalding hot water came out of a cold water tap – and the trunk in little Mandy's room that everyone tried in vain to open, only to find it opened easily half an hour later.

Once, but only once, the shop assistant Miss Janet Harrop babysat for Carol and her husband. Late at night she heard the downstairs door rattle and then she heard noises in the backyard. She was sure the place was being broken into yet nothing else happened and there was no trace of any disturbance in the yard.

Other curious and unexplained incidents, small in themselves but adding up to a formidable total, resulted in Carol and Janet being reluctant to work in the shop during the hours of darkness. Curiously enough the odd happenings seemed to come to an end after about six months. A couple of months later the Payne family moved to Macclesfield and I have heard no more about the ghost of the hanged man.

Heaton Chapel, Stockport, GREATER MANCHESTER

A large and old building, No. 412 Manchester Road, is thought to have had a long and sinister history and to be haunted.

During the First World War the property was occupied by a Polish family; one of the little girls of the family now lives quietly in the Manchester area but she still remembers vividly some of the experiences she and her family had in the house at Heaton Chapel.

The family had a cousin who was private secretary to the Emperor Franz Joseph of Austria and before the War they had acquired land and property around Manchester. They settled into the house in Manchester Road in 1914.

One night, soon after they had settled in, this teenaged Polish girl was preparing for bed when she was astonished to see a vanity box on the dressing-table opening and closing by itself; then one night she suddenly found herself awake and saw a black figure with a grotesque and ugly face, screeching words at her that sounded like 'Try and find me . . . come on . . . try and find me . . .' The terrified girl awakened her sister who was sleeping with her but by the time she was awake the figure had disappeared.

However on 'many other occasions', this witness told the *Stockport Express* in December 1974, she and another sister saw the same form, about six feet in height with a dark, pointed face, walking down the stairs carrying a lantern. They noticed that each step the figure took seemed to be accompanied by the sound of a trotting horse. Sometimes the sisters would follow the figure down into the cellars where it always disappeared into one of the walls after pausing beside a well. One morning the girls' father, a practical and hard-headed Polish businessman, was lying in bed looking out of the window when the bedclothes were mysteriously drawn off him. There was no other person in the room at the time.

Some sort of reason and cause for the haunting was provided by an elderly shopkeeper and neighbour, a Mrs Birch, who had a considerable knowledge of the history of Heaton Chapel. She said that years earlier, when the railway through Heaton Chapel was being laid, scores of Irish labourers were brought over to do the heavy work; they were little less than criminals, drunk for most of the time and always in trouble with the police. They brought over with them a party of prostitutes who were almost as bad as the men. When the work was finished, after a period of two or three years, the men left the area but no one seemed to trouble about the prostitutes or their children. One of the houses used by the labourers was the house in Manchester Road and after they had gone the authorities moved in to clear up the place. When they set about laying a new floor they found the bones of human babies buried almost at ground level . . . and still the question remained, what had happened to the prostitutes? Mrs Birch always said, 'Human bones will be unearthed when the house is eventually demolished. The babies' bones were found at ground level; what about the cellar and what about the well?'

The dark figure seen at the house on many occasions, sometimes in one of the bedrooms but more frequently on the stairs, is thought to be the murderer who killed the prostitutes' children and probably the prostitutes too. There is an old belief that says the unquiet spirit of a murderer always returns to the scene of the crime.

Heaton Norris, Stockport, GREATER MANCHESTER

On 17 March 1969, lorry driver George Wilshaw saw a giant male figure dressed in black in the back garden of his home in Providence Street, Heaton Norris.

It was about four o'clock in the morning that George opened the back door of his terraced house and walked the ten yards to the outside toilet. As he opened the door to return he saw in the clear moonlight a massive male figure standing under a tree that separated his garden from that of his neighbour. The figure appeared to be dressed entirely in black and made only slight movements. George did not recognize the face, but afterwards he was certain that the figure was aware of his presence.

Puzzled and not a little annoyed at someone being in his garden at that hour and causing him something of a shock, he called out to ask what the fellow wanted and what was he doing there. When there was no reply George stormed over towards the figure but when he had almost reached it, perhaps only five feet away, the form completely vanished.

Thinking that the man must have eluded him somehow and deciding that he was dealing with someone who was up to no good, George ran into the house, armed himself with a heavy poker, and came out to search for the intruder. 'I walked round the backyard looking everywhere,' he said, 'checking the old air raid shelters and the toilets to see if I could find the man I had seen. I found nothing and I heard not a single sound, not even when the figure vanished in front of my eyes.'

That evening George Wilshaw (who later moved to Morgan Place, Heaton Norris) and his wife were sitting watching television when their pet dog whimpered to go outside. George opened the back door and the dog took one look outside and froze, the hair on its back rising. Then it cried loudly and bolted back into the house. George hurriedly shut and bolted the door!

For no less than three days the dog was in a state of terror and distress; it refused to leave the house for a moment and would not go near the back door. Then George saw the figure again.

He was awakened early that morning at about the same time as previously and with some hesitation he made his way to the outside toilet, looking round carefully to notice anything vaguely unfamiliar in the dawn light. As before, he was on his way back to the house when he saw the same gigantic figure, black and silent, but this time it stood near to his neighbour's coal shed.

Again George called out to the figure, asking what he wanted and again there was no response. This time George was determined to find out who or what it was and, keeping his eyes on the black figure, George ran straight towards it and again, when he was within a few feet of the figure, it disappeared in front of his eyes. As before there was no hurried movement and no sound at all. The figure seemed to turn its head towards the neighbour's house and then it was simply no longer there. When he returned home from work that day George learned that his neighbour had died suddenly.

Discussing the strange experience later George Wilshaw stressed the fact that he had not been drinking on either occasion, he certainly was not dreaming and it was no imagination. Looking back on the affair he felt it was difficult to accept as coincidence the appearance of the figure and the sudden death of the neighbour. 'And there is the size of the thing . . . that figure was at least half as big again as me. In my whole life I have never seen a human being as big . . . something must have possessed me to make an attack on it!'

The terraced houses of Providence Street, Heaton Norris, were demolished in 1971.

Hey Houses, near Lytham St Annes, LANCASHIRE

A block of neo-Georgian flats now occupies the site of Fancy Lodge, a charming – and haunted – thatched cottage that dated from the seventeenth century. A mysterious 'lady in white' was repeatedly seen by passers-by, a figure that disappeared when it was approached or spoken to.

An ancient property nearby, 'The Elms', was partly haunted (the property was subsequently divided into two dwellings) by a presence that floated down the stairs, hovered in the hallway causing the temperature to become appreciably colder, and set the family dog growling.

Hollinwood, near Oldham, GREATER MANCHESTER

Ferranti's Avenue Works factory now occupies part of the site of an old estate known as Birchen Bower, an estate that once had an eccentric owner, Miss Hannah Beswick, whose body, on her instructions, was embalmed, preserved unburied by her physician and returned to her old home for a week every twenty-one years. There is evidence to suggest that the restless ghost of Hannah Beswick haunted several parts of the estate and several properties both before and after the body was eventually laid to rest more than a hundred years after her death. Curious disturbances, including a shadowy figure, in the vicinity of the transformer department of the new Ferranti factory in April 1956, were attributed to this strange and unsettled ghost.

Hannah Beswick inherited Birchen Bower Farm from her wealthy half-brother John Beswick when he died at the early age of thirty-three in 1737. Hannah, two years older than John, took over the running of the farm and efficiently managed the estate as well as other properties and estates at Cheetwood, Ashton-under-Lyne, Wakefield and Bradford which she also inherited. For some years she lived quietly in the four-gabled house built in the form of a cross and then, in 1745, came the Jacobite rebellion and reports that 'Bonnie' Prince Charlie and his rebels were approaching Manchester. Looting and stealing was rife and Hannah, in fear for her money and valuables, buried her fortune and many of her possessions in and around Birchen Bower. There was nothing wrong with hiding valuables in time of trouble but when all danger had passed Hannah resolutely left her treasures and her money where she had hidden them and could never be induced to reveal their whereabouts.

As the years passed her health deteriorated and at length she left Birchen Bower and moved to a small cottage by a mill-stream where she lived for the rest of her life, alone and happy in her isolation that was only punctuated by occasional visits from relations (still trying to discover the location of the family fortune) and regular visits from a young surgeon from Manchester, Charles White, who became something of a confidant and friend as well as a skilful physician who, according to Thomas De Quincey (1785-1859) did much to alleviate his patients' sufferings.

In 1758, when she was fifty-six, Hannah realized that her end was in sight and she promised to show her relations where she had hidden her money and her valuables if they would take her once more to Birchen Bower. To their lasting regret they let things slide and the eccentric heiress became too ill to be moved from her last home. That same year she died, taking the secret of her hidden treasure with her.

One of Hannah Beswick's secret fears had long been the dread of being accidentally buried alive – a not infrequent occurrence in the days when cataleptic conditions were imperfectly understood – and it would appear that she left a legacy of £25,000 to Charles White on condition that he kept her 'out of the ground' and when, beyond all doubt, death had taken place, that the body was embalmed as perfectly as possible. There is also a tradition that Birchen Bower itself was made over to the surgeon, subject to the same conditions, although Hannah's will, made shortly before her death, mentions only a bequest of £100 to Charles White with the estate of Birchen Bower to a cousin on her mother's side, then to the cousin's daughter and then to Charles White. In fact both ladies predeceased the surgeon so that he did indeed become possessed of the estate.

A letter, written by one of the trustees the year Hannah died, leaves no doubt that it was understood by the executrices and by Charles White that her body was to be embalmed and White, then thirty years old, proceeded to remove the entrails and some of the bones, preserve the flesh with arsenic, alcohol, camphor and oils and complete the embalming process with resin, saltpetre and aromatics, finally swathing the whole body, except the face, with strong bandages.

The mummy of Hannah Beswick was taken to Cheetwood Old House, the ancestral home of the Beswicks, and there it remained for two years, watched over by the two executrices as required by Hannah's last will and testament. Then White took possession of the mummy and kept it for years at his home in King Street, Manchester, in the case of a grandfather clock from which the clock face and works had been removed. The old woman's head showed where a clock-face had once been, screened from view by a white velvet veil that (according to De Quincey who saw the mummy in the clockcase) was withdrawn once a year in the presence of two witnesses in accordance with Hannah Beswick's dying wishes.

On his retirement from medical practice White took the mummy in its case to his country residence at Sale in Cheshire. Meanwhile, strange happenings were being reported from Birchen Bower. Not only were odd noises heard, causing peculiar behaviour by the farm animals, but there were also growing reports of a figure thought to be the ghost of Hannah Beswick, wandering about her former home. In particular it was noticed that these disturbances and sightings corresponded with every seventh anniversary of Hannah's death.

Local tradition has it that another curious condition, laid down by the eccentric Hannah, was an agreement that once every twenty-one years her body should reside for seven days at Birchen Bowers and it seems more than likely that the zealous Charles White, something of an eccentric himself it would seem, did indeed convey the mummified body of Hannah Beswick to Birchen Bowers in accordance with the contract he had undertaken. At the old farmhouse the mummy usually spent the seven days in the granary and on the morning that it was fetched away it was often noticed that the cattle were loose in their stalls. On one occasion a cow was found up in the hayloft; how it had managed to get there remained a complete mystery.

As the years passed Birchen Bowers became divided into several separate dwelling places and the various occupants, chiefly handloom weavers, often reported hearing the rustle of 'Madame Beswick's' ghost as it flitted along a corridor or stairway. Sometimes a form was seen, a lady in a black silk gown that would be noticed near the front entrance or maybe gliding through the parlour of one of the other ground-floor rooms and always it seemed to vanish at the spot where an oddly shaped flagstone stood out among its regular-shaped companions.

From time to time Hannah's relatives and others surreptitiously sought to locate the old lady's treasure but there is only one report of any of it ever being found. At the end of the eighteenth century a weaver prized up part of the old parlour flooring to enable him to erect a loom and found a tin filled with gold. He told no one of his find and sold the gold, piece by piece, to a jeweller in Manchester, and the tin that had contained the treasure was preserved in his family for several generations.

Meanwhile Hannah's ghost was still seen occasionally and Charles White lived on in retirement at 'The Priory', Sale, a keen collector of anatomical subjects and other curios. When he was eighty he presented his anatomical collection to St Mary's Hospital, Manchester, but not the mummy of Hannah Beswick, which he put out of sight in the loft of his home. On White's death in 1813, Dr Oliver, the physician who had attended White in his last illness, found the mummy and a few other curios bequeathed to him and he in turn left the mummy and various other objects to the Manchester Natural History Society, for their museum. There the mummy, out of its grandfather clock casing and enclosed in a glass case, proved a popular attraction for many years, labelled simply, 'The mummy of Miss Beswick'. A visitor to the museum in 1850 described the exhibit as follows: 'The body was well preserved but the face was shrivelled and black. The legs and trunk were wrapped in a strong cloth such as is used for bed-ticks, and the body was that of a little woman. It was in a glass coffin-shaped case.'

In 1868 the Natural History Society's museum was incorporated with the newly-formed Owen's College and the college commissioners tried to find Hannah's descendants so that they could get rid of the disintegrating body but no one wanted it. No records pertaining to the mummy have been preserved and information concerning it became vague and inaccurate; during the last few years that it was on show in the Natural History Museum visitors were told that it was the body of a Manchester woman who had given a sum of money to charity on condition that her body was never buried. There was not even a death certificate and eventually the Home Secretary granted permission for the unwanted body of Hannah Beswick to be laid to rest in Harpurhey Cemetery, Manchester, where it was accordingly buried on 22 July 1868, one-hundred-and-ten years after her death. Still the restless ghost of Hannah was reputed to walk at Birchen Bowers, both within the converted house and in the grounds, in 'The Priory' where the mummy had been kept for years by Charles White and in particular in the vicinity of an old barn on the former Beswick estate that bore the engraved monogram of the Beswick family. Here, when most of Birchen Bower house had been demolished, many and varied manifestations were reported from many sources. Strange lights, alarming noises and the inevitable form of a little old lady wandering among the surroundings that she had known and loved . . . such stories cropped up repeatedly until the estate disappeared beneath the twentieth-century factories and even then no less than thirty-five Ferranti workers claimed, in 1956, to have seen or heard a ghost that could be that of Hannah Beswick, a sad, eccentric and strangely restless ghost.

Hoylake, MERSEYSIDE

The old Royal Hotel that was built in 1797 facing the Irish Sea was reputed to be haunted by the ghost of a man in Norfolk jacket, knickerbockers and a tweed cap.

Some years ago the proprietor at the time told me of frequent reports of appearances of the unidentified ghost in one particular wing of the hotel. One of the female staff members said she had several times seen a male figure in tweeds walk down the corridor from the hall to the ballroom and she described the figure as 'slight but energetic and lively'. Twice she followed the mysterious figure but each time it disappeared inexplicably. Looking back on the experiences she realized that she had not noticed any sound accompanying the appearance. A barman said he saw a figure answering the same description pass from the billiards room and disappear along the corridor where the same form was seen by a colleague. The figure passed through the room where the barman stood; it appeared to be solid and natural in every way and although he did not notice any sound accompanying the 'brown knickerbockered and tweeds' figure, he did not think that the experience was in fact soundless.

A maintenance joiner on the hotel staff said he saw, many times, a similar figure in the same room. Other apparently psychic disturbances at the old Royal included the opening and closing of doors and unexplained footsteps. An old Hoylake superstition, probably based on some long-forgotten experience, says that anyone finding a drowned body in the sea must ensure that it is given Christian burial for whoever puts such a body back into the sea will forever be haunted by the ghost of the drowned person.

Hurst Green, near Blackburn, LANCASHIRE

The pleasant landscape hereabouts was well known to Ned King, the eighteenth-century highwayman. His favourite hunting ground was the ancient highway that still runs through Hurst Green, and he made his headquarters in a loft over a barn in premises where the Punch Bowl Inn now stands.

So successful was this Lancashire Dick Turpin that he acquired the nickname of 'The Phantom', so cleverly did he seem to vanish into the darkness and cover his tracks to elude capture. One reason for his success was that he was in league with the local landlord who took a cut of his 'earnings'. Ned's method was to conceal himself in the hayloft and select his victims as they left the inn, according to their appearance.

Some way along the road the selected traveller would be stopped and relieved of his money and valuables. Back Ned would go to the inn where the landlord would take his share and Ned would conceal himself for the next victim.

Gradually the authorities began to realize that the highwayman's activities centred on the Punch Bowl Inn and one dark night when Ned returned to his loft the building was surrounded and he was called upon to surrender. Ned put up a fight but he was soon overwhelmed on a gallery and captured. Soon afterwards he was hanged and gibbetted in nearby Gallows Lane.

For more than a century after his death Ned's ghost troubled the inn, throwing things about, making a lot of noise and, occasionally, showing himself on the minstrel's balcony where he was captured. In 1942 a priest from Stonyhurst College carried out a service of exorcism and things were quiet for a time but at the end of 1973 the licensee, John Davies, said he noticed many strange happenings: the sound of running footsteps, strange moaning sounds that seemed to come from the old beams and the totally inexplicable movement of objects. When I was there in March 1977 one of the staff told me that the delightful atmosphere of the inn during the hours of daylight often changed after dark when an eerie, watching and expectant influence seemed to pervade the old inn.

Hyde, GREATER MANCHESTER

Hyde Lads Club was reported to be haunted in 1968 by the sound of clicking billiard balls that emanated from a deserted billiards room at the dead of night.

The club leader, Andre Davis, who had taken over the boys' club a year earlier, said he and his wife Ann would lie in bed listening to the sounds night after night. No one would be in the billiards room, situated over their bedroom, but they would wait, knowing that before they could get to sleep there would be a sudden crash, as if a table had been thrown from the ceiling, and then there would be the 'click-click' of billiard balls, sometimes lasting for nearly half an hour, sometimes for only a few minutes.

When they first heard the noises Andre would take his labrador dog and go towards the stairs leading to the upper floor, but at the stairs the dog would stop, its hair bristling, and refuse to go any further. When Andre went on up the stairs by himself he always found the room completely deserted.

The mystery began on the first night Andre slept in the building. That time he heard nothing but thought he would take a look round before settling down for the night. As he went into the billiards room he saw an old man playing by himself. The man seemed to look up and then he continued with his game. Andre looked all round the room and when he looked back the man had disappeared and the billiards table was covered. Later he learned that an old club leader died while playing billiards in the club and as he fell he brought down a lot of workmen's materials.

Finally, and to Andre Davis the most astonishing thing about the whole series of mysterious happenings, was the fact that every morning after he had heard the ghostly billiard player, a clock, given in memory of the old club leader, was found going backwards!

The couple of miles between Hyde and Mottram in Longdendale is the haunt of a phantom lorry, according to reports of curious incidents and experiences over the years.

The story of the phantom lorry seems to have been born following an unfortunate road accident when a man lost his life. The coroner at the subsequent inquest was not satisfied and he took his jury to the scene at midnight in an attempt to find a logical explanation for the circumstances surrounding the fatality. The difficulty was that a man swore he had seen a lorry backing out of a side turning or entrance and that lorry, he said, had been the cause of the accident – but there was no opening of any kind at that particular point of the road and furthermore, as far as could be established, there had been no lorry.

The coroner himself, a practical and painstaking individual, the late Mr Stuart Rodger, had used the expression 'phantom lorry' in February 1930 during the course of the inquest on a twenty-nine-year-old bus driver, Charles Ridgway, who came from Hyde.

Ridgway had been on the back of his cousin's motor-cycle at the time and early in the morning both men were discovered in the road badly injured; Ridgway died without recovering consciousness but his cousin, Albert Collinson, survived a fractured skull. There were no witnesses but Collinson asserted that as he approached a side opening between an inn and a cross-roads a large lorry had suddenly backed into the road in front of him.

Police officials and local administrators pointed out that there was no opening of any kind and the police could find no evidence or tracks of a lorry. Yet Collinson was adamant and he said he definitely recalled seeing the 'jagged edge of the lorry' before the motor-cycle crash.

The affair was never satisfactorily concluded and local people pointed out that this was by no means the only mysterious accident on this stretch of road. On the contrary, during the previous twenty-two months no less than sixteen accidents had taken place there involving cars, lorries, motor-cycles and pedestrians, resulting in three deaths, twenty-five people being injured and eighteen vehicles badly damaged. In every case, the coroner said, there was no satisfactory explanation. Yet the road had a good surface and was almost straight.

Residents came forward to report other curious incidents: footsteps in the roadway when it was deserted and plainly devoid of any person or traffic; a fierce dog that was present when the footsteps passed returned to its owner, cowed, howling with fright and obviously terrified. The licensee of the nearby inn, Mr William Gratton, said he had heard footsteps for which he could find no explanation so frequently that he had ceased to be alarmed but another resident was very frightened and used to scream when she was awakened in the night by the loud noises which had no obvious explanation, noises which sounded like a heavily built man walking up and down the roadway. What really frightened her was the fact that she had noticed the sounds almost invariably preceded a crash on the road.

Psychic research investigators visited the area and explored every possible theory. They walked over the stretch of haunted road at all hours; they tested the idea that fluttering strips of paper caught in the hedge might be picked up in a car's headlights and cause the driver to swerve alarmingly; they looked into the possibility that the squeaking from a nearby revolving windmill set over a well could sound like a heavy vehicle braking; they examined the likelihood of a sloping hedge and a jutting wall being mistaken for a heavy lorry backing into the road at night or in mist. But none of these ideas, either individually or collectively, could satisfactorily account for all the evidence for strange happenings.

The police, prosaic to the last, said the whole trouble was that motorists and other road users drove too fast on that stretch of road and gradually the affair died down, only to be renewed less than a year later when another series of accidents took place in the same vicinity.

This time a six-wheeled pantechnicon ran into a lamp-standard; a motor-cyclist was thrown head-first over a hedge; two cars collided on a wide stretch of the road and a pedestrian was run down by a lorry that approached silently and suddenly in front of him and then disappeared.

Shortly afterwards a local driver who knew the road and always drove along it with extreme caution crashed into a hedge; he said he was unable to control his vehicle which veered to the right in spite of his efforts to drive straight, yet it was subsequently established that there was nothing mechanically wrong with the car.

Later a young grocer from Hyde was found lying beside his bicycle two hundred yards from the spot where the 'phantom lorry' was said to appear and he died without being able to give an account of what had happened; again there were no witnesses.

The police began to keep a constant watch on the road and eventually the wall and hedge that some people thought resembled a lorry were removed and although there are still accidents and occasional reports of curious happenings in the area there certainly has not been the continuous string of accidents that haunted the road in the early 1930s.

Kirkham, The Fylde, LANCASHIRE

Five miles north of Kirkham, in the parish of Medlar-with-Wesham, stands Mowbreck Hall, for centuries the home of the Westby family and the scene of a ghastly visitation: a gory head. Many people claim to have seen this singular apparition in the private chapel at Mowbreck, especially about midnight at Hallowe'en, the night that it was first seen.

Vivian Haydock was a Roman Catholic priest who was connected by marriage to the Westbys and in 1583, notwithstanding the law and the new religion of the Queen, he was robed and ready to perform Mass on the Feast of All Hallows when a vision suddenly appeared above the altar. Haydock's son George, also a priest, was in London but in no immediate danger as far as his father knew; in fact he had been betrayed. As Haydock began to intone the words of the Mass he saw floating before him a horrifying sight: his son's head, bruised and bleeding. Vivian Haydock collapsed with shock and died soon afterwards. His son George was already confined in the Tower and the following year he was hanged, drawn and quartered. His head was preserved for a time at Cottam Hall, the home of the Haydocks, and was then transferred to Lane End House, Mawdesley, the home of Thomas Finch who had married a Haydock, and there it remains to this day.

There are those who dispute that the head in the glass case is that of George Haydock, some maintaining that it is that of William Haydock, a Cistercian monk hanged in 1537. Be that as it may visitors to Mowbreck over the years have sometimes asserted that they have momentarily glimpsed the form of a bloodstained and dripping priest's head hovering with gaping mouth above the chapel altar.

In the 1960s Mowbreck Hall became a country club and the proprietors were among those who asserted that they heard weird noises, unexplained footsteps and loud groans that worried them. It was also asserted that articles moved by themselves and not infrequently disappeared completely and then reappeared in a different place. The club and restaurant closed in 1970 and over a period of several years the place was nearly wrecked by vandals.

The Bell and Bottle on the Kirkham by-pass has long been reputed to harbour at least two ghosts, possibly the victims of two tragedies that are supposed to have taken place here long, long ago. One ghost walks along the 'haunted corridor' but no one knows the circumstances that may have surrounded this death; it may even have taken place at the spot where the apparition is seen or there may once have been a room or a cupboard where now there is a corridor. The other death is said to have been that of a stable boy, accidentally kicked to death by a horse when the present restaurant was a stable, and here a wispy, half-formed figure of a sad-faced boy in old-fashioned clothes has been seen within the last few years. It is here that some previous owners asserted that their dogs repeatedly showed signs of fear, although nothing was visible to their human companions.

Kirkby, MERSEYSIDE

A block of new town flats at Tedbury Close, Southdene, housed six families; in August 1971 one family was rehoused and the other five refused to pay their rents because, they said, they were terrified by ghostly manifestations.

One of the residents, twenty-eight-year-old Mrs Elsie Gill, found life so insufferable that she and her eight-year-old daughter, Elaine, and six-year-old twins moved to another house across the road. Mrs Gill said at the time that the trouble began eight months earlier when the temperature throughout the whole flat suddenly dropped alarmingly; even the cat started to howl. Mrs Gill said she looked towards the fireplace and saw the figures of two small children standing there looking at her and a tall adult standing by the door. She screamed and they all vanished. After that experience she and each of her three children saw one or another of these figures regularly. The children were so frightened that they all insisted on sleeping in one room with their mother. One morning, at about two o'clock, Mrs Gill heard the sound of laughing and joking coming from the direction of the back bedroom and when she cautiously opened the door of that room she saw the figure of one of the children she had seen before, jumping up and down on the bed.

One of the top flats was occupied by a family who stayed less than a weekend; they were replaced by Mr and Mrs Melia and their two-year-old son. Irene Melia was expecting another child at the time the family moved in so the neighbours decided not to mention the ghosts but on the very day of the move Mrs Melia's brother stayed overnight and suddenly found himself awake in the middle of the night and he saw a figure of a man in the room clutching a hatchet! Within a few days the Melia's little boy appeared to be playing with a phantom baby and several times they heard the sound of a baby crying when no real baby was anywhere in the area.

This 'phantom baby' was also heard by Mrs Pat Nugent, her husband and their three children who lived on the ground floor of the same block. Mr and Mrs Michael Becket and their four children lived on the first floor and they reported having seen a greyish figure outside their doorway which they could not explain. The occupants of a top flat, Mrs Ethel Conchie, her brother and four children, said they had seen the ghost of a boy wearing an Eton-style collar, and one of the younger sisters, nineteen-year-old Irene, stated that she saw a ghost in the flat no less than six times and on four of those times she fainted with the shock.

A ground-floor flat occupant, Mr Chris Hamill, said at the time, 'It's been going on for about two years and for a long time people who saw things were frightened to speak about it in case everyone else thought they were imagining things, but eventually it all came out and nearly everyone had some ghostly experience to relate'. Later there were reports of furniture being moved; moaning and wailing noises being heard at night; footsteps; doors opening and closing, and various other curious and apparently inexplicable happenings.

A local Roman Catholic priest blessed the flats; a spiritualist medium said he thought the appearances were a warning of some future tragedy and the responsible authority at that time, Liverpool Corporation, said they would seek the advice of people knowledgeable in such matters and try to do the best they could for the people concerned.

In answer to my enquiry as to how the matter ended the City of Liverpool Housing Department informed me in March 1977 that with the reorganization of local government in 1974 responsibility for housing in the Kirkby area passed to the newly established Knowsley Borough Council and members of the Housing Department staff and records also passed to the new council. My enquiries in that direction resulted in a most helpful letter from Mr Alex Grant, Chairman of the Kirkby Local History Society, who visited Tedbury Close and found the 'haunted' premises occupied. He tells me that 'the original tenants did withhold their rents and various priests and other people visited the place but the occupants were in such fear that the families were rehoused.'

On my behalf Alex Grant spoke to a local electrician, Frank Morriss, who remembers the affair with some amusement since he was sent along to repair the lighting that had failed on the dark stairway. When he arrived a group of hysterical women were gathered around the entrance to the flats, and they begged him not to enter; one lady swore that her husband had been thrown down the stairs only the night before by 'something' that was tremendously strong and, according to him, had only one eye. Frank grinned and went up the stairs with confidence, for as a young boy he used to stoke up the boilers at night on his own in Liverpool's St Nicholas Church. To reach those boilers he had to pass through the crypt surrounded by the remains of corpses from long ago. Frank fixed the lights at Tedbury Close without difficulty and came down again without encountering any ghost, but it was a wild and blustery night and to some extent he could understand the women's fears.

Alex Grant also spoke to some old residents of Kirkby who remember when the area was really rural and completely isolated from Liverpool. Certainly some of the very old folk would not venture anywhere near the Southdene area after dark on account of a ghost that was said to lurk often around the hedge of the old farm, where it was reputed an old farmer had thrown himself down a well at his farm. That farm occupies the site of the present Tedbury Close.

Lancaster, LANCASHIRE

Now the club house of Lancaster Golf Club, Jacobean Ashton Hall has seen sudden death and great unhappiness, frantic priests and anxious damsels, a ghostly White Lady and a legend to account for it.

It is said that long ago a jealous lord of Ashton, before he set off for the wars, ordered that his lady was to be restrained in the tower of the Hall until his return, for he did not trust her to preserve her virtue. He was delayed and when he arrived back at Ashton his lady was dead; thereafter, it is said, her mournful ghost has been seen walking round and round the tower – her prison that became her tomb – on windswept, moonlit nights.

Leyland, near Preston, LANCASHIRE

Runshaw House has long been reputed to be haunted by the ghost of a grey-haired woman dressed in black. The ghost is common knowledge to many local people and there are numerous stories of such a figure, some say wearing a white blouse or top, floating or drifting through one of the upper rooms and disappearing into an outer wall. Who she is or why she walks nobody knows. The figure seems to have been especially active during the several years that the house was empty between 1971 and 1975. Dunshaw College now occupies Runshaw House and the principal tells me that to the best of his knowledge the place is 'entirely unsupplied with ghosts'. Nearby Runshaw Hall is a Roman Catholic home for the handicapped.

Littleborough, GREATER MANCHESTER

Historic Townhouse, dating from 1798, owes its name to the del Tons, a very ancient family whose name occurs again and again in local records; there is for instance William del Ton, one of the last of the Saxon families of standing who resisted the raiding forces of Norsemen and a court roll of 1336 carries the name of Matilda, wife of Peter del Ton. It is generally accepted that Townhouse was the first house in the district and surely it is appropriate that such an historic house should have not one ghost but two.

One ghost is known as 'Lady Margaret' and the other more affectionately as 'Janie' and their activities, irregular and varied as they are, have been reported by many tenants as well as the successive owners. Mr Harold Howarth, the present owner of the property, which was left to him by his parents, tells me he found the sixty-four roomed house too big to live in and so he made it into luxury flats, while he has a delightful bungalow in the grounds. During the alterations to the house none of the workers would be in the house alone when it began to get dark.

Although Mr Howarth has never seen either of the ghosts he has no doubt about their authenticity. He says 'Janie' seemed to be about thirty-five and always appeared in white.

'She appears from time to time and is a most friendly person. There was a German lady who lived there and she became quite accustomed to frequent visits by the ghost.' Once 'Janie' was seen near the front door and a tenant, taking her for a real person, said 'Good morning' and then found that 'Janie' had disappeared. This ghost was seen quite recently, Mr Howarth tells me, and sometimes those who see her say that she wears something like a key round her neck and that she nearly always smiles.

Mrs Kay Reynolds, a tenant at Townhouse, gave a vivid description of the 'Lady Margaret' ghost after she saw the apparition in 1971. Mrs Reynolds was in the lounge of her flat one afternoon doing some dusting. She had just picked up her knitting when she turned and realized that a certain vase was not where it should be and then she saw a dark figure standing with one hand on her hip and the other down by her side, almost hidden in the folds of her dress.

The feature that stood out in Mrs Reynolds's mind was the heavy bracelet that 'Lady Margaret' wore. The figure was tall, square-shouldered and slim-waisted. 'The thing that really surprised me,' she said in 1972, 'was that I always thought ghosts were transparent but this one looked solid enough and she must have been solid because by standing where she did she hid my vase!'

Mrs Reynolds thought the ghost was visible for perhaps two minutes. 'There was definitely something there, there is no doubt about it. I saw her once more, or thought I did, in the corridor but it was not nearly as clear as the first time.'

The area of the cellars of Townhouse is said to have a strange atmosphere and many people have the feeling down there that they are being watched. There are stories of a secret passage running from Townhouse to Stubley Old Hall but Mr Howarth tells me he has never seen any sign of it and if there is one it must be bricked-up. Secret passages or not, Townhouse deserves a ghost or two and I feel I know what Mr Howarth means when he says: 'I have not seen either ghost but I know there is something there.'

Liverpool, MERSEYSIDE

Penny Lane was made famous by the Beatles; another phenomenon of the area is the unseen ghost of number 44. In 1971 the two printers who owned the premises began to hear about strange noises emanating from the empty shop, especially at weekends. A thorough investigation included taking up floorboards, examining walls and roof and printing machinery, but no explanation was found for the sounds of pacing footsteps that kept neighbours awake and so disturbed them that they twice called the police. When a recording apparatus was left running one night, sounds of banging and shuffling were recorded. The police asserted that there was no evidence of rats or mice and no intruder was ever apprehended.

The old ornamental gardens at Rivington are thought to be haunted by one of Liverpool's famous sons, Lord Leverhulme, who lived in the bungalow and was responsible for building the gardens. More than one visitor has reported seeing a small man, dressed in a gold-check maroon suit, walking down steps in the old bungalow grounds; a figure that vanishes when it reaches the bottom of the steps.

One witness, a local man who knows the place well, said in 1975 that there was no normal way in which the man he saw could have disappeared from his sight. So puzzled was he that he spent some time searching the whole area.

Lord Leverhulme was born in Wood Street in 1851 and died in 1925. He began his career as a grocer and went on to found the commercial empire of Unilever. Other people have seen the silver-haired and well-dressed figure, often on bright, sunny days; it always disappears at the same spot and it is always seen walking down the same steps.

Knotty Ash is well-known as the home of Ken Dodd, the brilliant and original comedian, who was born in Liverpool and was once frightened by a very curious happening at his beautiful Georgian farmhouse home. He was sitting comfortably in his sitting-room, relaxed and happy, when something caught his eye and looking up he saw a disembodied arm floating in through the door that leads to the kitchen. The hand was cupped as if it were reaching for a glass. The room seemed to become dim and at first Ken thought it was his father and he called out but there was no reply. Suddenly he felt the outstretched hand was reaching towards him and he jumped out of his chair and dashed upstairs. He never saw the same thing again but he refuses to explain the experience in terms of imagination. 'The whole thing was quite real and solid,' he will tell you. 'I was scared out of my wits.'

The area of Lodge Lane, Liverpool, was reported to be haunted in 1974; haunted by the ghost of a girl who was murdered there.

Twenty-eight-year-old Carol McLean, dark-skinned, dark-eyed and beautiful, opened the door of her flat one afternoon to a young man and his girl-friend. Later, at Liverpool Crown Court, the couple pleaded guilty to murdering Carol; they had expected to find upwards of £200 in the flat but they only found a few coins. They battered her with a hammer and then stabbed her in the chest with a kitchen knife. As the two cold-blooded killers started their life sentences the neighbours were talking of a new terror in their street, for some of the people who used to hear the tap-tap of Carol's high heels as she regularly made her way home around midnight claimed that they could still hear the footsteps at the same time each night.

One young couple who lived only a hundred yards from Carol's flat said they were terrified. The girl said Carol once asked her to try to listen until she heard her safely home and agreed to this, for Carol worked late in some of the tougher clubs. Night after night this neighbour said she and her husband used to lie awake until they heard Carol's unmistakable footsteps pass their house and retreat to the door of her flat. After she was dead, they said, they still heard the footsteps clearly and distinctly, almost every night. Often they would be asleep by midnight, only to be woken up by the sound of Carol's individual tap-tap-tap. Many times they jumped out of bed and went to the window but the street was always deserted and by then the footsteps had ceased.

During the Second World War a respected policeman was among hundreds of people killed in the area of Lawrence Gardens during the German bombing raids. Oblivious of his own safety, he regularly patrolled the vicinity and it was there that he was blown to pieces as he made his way along the pitch-black roads, feeling his way by tapping his truncheon on walls, railings and doors. In the early 1970s several residents reported seeing the figure of a policeman in old-fashioned uniform, wearing a kind of haversack on his back with a tin helmet strapped to it, making his way along the darkening streets, tapping his truncheon on walls and railings as he passed. Whenever those who saw the phantom policeman tried to catch up with or pass 'him', the figure inexplicably disappeared.

Longridge, near Preston, LANCASHIRE

Off the Dilworth Road, on the lane running north that leads to Nook Fold, there is a slab of stone, nearly two-and-a-half metres long, nestling beneath a holly hedge. It is a stone that is reputed to have imprisoned a troublesome ghost – or boggart – for more than three hundred years.

The inscription is still plainly visible:

RAVFFE : RADCLIFFE : LAID : THIS
STONE : TO : LYE : FOR : EVER : A : D : 1655

Tradition has overlaid legend that replaced the true story of The Written Stone, as it has been called for centuries, but it seems that the area hereabouts was haunted by a nefarious and spiteful ghost, a 'boggart' that molested lonely travellers, scratching, pinching and punching any solitary wayfarer. It was also said to be responsible for frightful noises, horrible bumping sounds and terrifying screeches; it was even reputed to have caused the death of at least one local inhabitant. A nearby farmhouse was occupied by a family named Radcliffe who seem to have been particularly plagued and it is a historical fact that several of Ralph Radcliffe's family died shortly before the date carved on the stone. A subsequent owner of the farmhouse decided to make use of the great slab of stone and he sent men and horses to shift it to his dairy. After several men and as many horses had toiled the whole day long – and there were many injuries to man and beast to remind folk of that day – the stone was at last set in the dairy but it seemed to be bewitched from the start: nothing could be placed on it without it falling over, it never settled and was forever causing crushed toes and nicked shins and anyone who sat on it was likely to be ill next day.

The farmer decided to put the stone back where it came from, hoping the boggart, or whatever it was associated with the stone, would leave his farm at the same time. He prepared for another hard day's work but strangely enough, the return journey was accomplished with great ease, in a quarter the time it took to remove it and only one horse was needed!

A local doctor is said to have poured scorn on the story of the haunted stone and he rode out to issue a challenge that he had prepared but when he came in sight of the stone his horse reared and a shapeless form seemed to rise from the stone and almost choke the life out of him; fortunately the horse found his feet, turned and plunged away down the lane taking the sceptical doctor to safety. Two miles on he managed to rein his horse to a stop and thereafter he never scoffed about The Written Stone and rarely talked of his experience.

Lostock, near Bolton, GREATER MANCHESTER

It is still possible to find the site of Lostock Tower, about four miles west of Bolton and once an important local residence, the home of the powerful Anderton family.

The neighbouring Heatons found themselves heavily in debt to the Andertons of the day, who were about to foreclose. The Heaton family managed to raise the money at the last moment and, late as it was on the last day that the debt was due, they rushed to the owner of the Tower, shouting that they had managed to raise the money. But Anderton of the Tower said the money should have been paid before sunset and refused to accept payment; next morning he said they were too late and declared the mortgage foreclosed.

The Heaton family was ruined and they never forgave Anderton; nor, it seems, did he escape retribution, for his 'soul' could not find rest and he was doomed to re-visit the scene of his cruelty on the anniversary of that fateful day. Furthermore, no horse belonging to an Anderton would ever cross a stream that led into the manor of Heaton. Retribution of a sort was achieved when Sir Francis Anderton lost his estates and died, childless and without heir.

Lytham, LANCASHIRE

The Ship and Royal inn has a ghost known affectionately as 'Charlie' although he is thought to be Squire John Talbot Clifton re-visiting his favourite hostelry. The form of a tall, thick-set and bearded man, wearing a long cloak and a tall hat, has been seen in the Mariners' Grill on the second floor. This was once the favourite bar of the handsome and jovial John Clifton who died in 1928 after a thousand adventures all over the world; the walls of this old inn must have heard them all a hundred times.

Occasionally a waitress or a customer will still notice a tall, dark figure at the far end of the Grill Room – a figure that disappears as quickly as it mysteriously appears – but more frequently these days odd happenings are credited to 'Charlie', such as the order that was recorded in a gruff voice on the meat suppliers' overnight answering service, although the order was written out at the inn and left on the desk ready for ordering; the inn's files that have been interfered with and muddled; the papers and other objects that have been moved and the 'curious atmosphere' that has been reported by more than one of the staff in certain parts of the old inn.

Lytham-St-Annes, LANCASHIRE

Lytham Hall, a seventeenth-century edifice, was partly destroyed by fire in the middle of the nineteenth century and restored with the present imposing Georgian frontage; it has a Long Gallery haunted by an unidentified White Lady who glides through the apartment and disappears at the far end. The figure was reported by staff and patients when the house was used as a convalescent centre during the Second World War and from time to time visitors still report odd experiences in this part of the building.

Two more unidentified ghosts have been seen on the top floor of the south wing, seemingly a very pleasant and light room, although a room with a strange atmosphere which becomes more apparent the longer one is in the room and especially when the evening shadows lengthen.

The Duke of Norfolk's Room, small and dark, has the reputation of being haunted by the sounds of heavy footsteps, clanking chains and a door that opens by itself.

Maghull, near Liverpool, MERSEYSIDE

Two or three miles north-west of Liverpool the southern part of the town of Maghull is reputedly haunted by the sounds of battle.

In 1648 the Royalist army passed this way as they fled south and there were skirmishes in the area; again in 1715 the Jacobites trying to escape when Preston was recaptured ran into trouble hereabouts. Either engagement may have left some kind of impression on the atmosphere that would account for the occasional and quite inexplicable sounds of galloping horses and the clash of arms that have been heard, usually at dusk, and also perhaps the forms of fleeing horsemen that have been seen some dawn mornings, near to an old grey stone wall that may have retained in some indefinable way a tragic, poignant and grave moment of forgotten history.

Manchester, GREATER MANCHESTER

The Shakespeare tavern in Fountain Street is reputed to harbour the ghostly presence of a young girl who died there more than a hundred years ago.

The story tells of a kitchen girl whose duties also included lighting and putting out the candles in the tavern. One night, exhausted after a long day of busy toil, she accidentally set fire to herself while snuffing out the candles and in running for help, she fell down the stairway and killed herself.

Now, it is said, her friendly ghost haunts The Shakespeare. A tavern with this name has stood on this site since 1771 and although the present premises are not that old the existing Tudor-style building was erected in the 1920s from the shell of a pub called The Shambles that had been dismantled at Chester.

Another story suggests that the servant girl slept in a small room entered from a flight of steps from the kitchen and that one night she accidentally set fire to herself and fell down these steps to her death. At all events members of the staff and customers have reported seeing the ghost of a girl in working clothes in the Lanchester Tavern's establishment and Mr Chris Connolly, the Assistant District Manager, has been good enough to supply me with some information and a photograph of this attractive tavern in the heart of the city centre.

There seems to be at least one other version of what may have happened. A chef is said to have attacked and raped a serving maid in the little room off the kitchen, an act for which he was hanged from a beam upstairs in the tavern where 'rope marks' are still to be seen. The ghost of this man is said to have haunted the upstairs rooms of the Shakespeare – or the premises that previously occupied the site – for something like three hundred years.

There used to be a rocking chair in the kitchen and certain members of the staff said that on occasions they had seen the chair moving back and forth of its own accord, but what connection, if any, there is between the rocking chair and the poor little serving girl or the lustful chef I have never been able to discover.

Some years ago an old curio shop known as the Rover's Return was reputedly haunted by a Jacobite ghost. The owner, Mr Francis Shaw, told me he had been aware of the ghost for more than ten years and that he and others had seen the phantom form.

Francis Shaw slept alone at the quaint fourteenth-century shop and the ghost often appeared at the foot of his bed. The figure, seemingly friendly and able to converse, told Francis Shaw that his name was James Stewart and that he travelled to Manchester with 'Bonnie' Prince Charlie and was stabbed to death in the house that became a shop.

Mr Robert Stark, an ex-Army man and a partner in the business, once stated that he slept alone in the shop on one occasion and heard loud crashing sounds from the direction of the cellar, but on examining the cellar he found nothing out of place and nothing to account for the noises.

The premises of Messrs Claridge, freight forwarders at Manchester Airport, were reported to be haunted by the ghost of an old man in 1971. Staff members and cleaners variously reported such a figure being seen sitting in a storeroom and also walking through an office and disappearing along a corridor; other employees reported incidents including strange noises, footsteps, a scream and the movement of office equipment.

The police were called in and one officer claimed to see the apparition and so did a lorry driver. The building was originally part of the barracks of a Manchester RAF Squadron and there was speculation at the time on the possibility that the ghost might date back to the war days.

In 1948 some steelworks at Trafford Park had a haunted crane. Footsteps were reported to sound on the roof of the crane when it was seventy feet above the ground and the crane driver, William Boardman, began to be worried. He had previously reported a defect in another crane and he thought the footsteps were those of the electrician, walking on his crane by mistake. He called out, 'You're on the wrong crane,' and when there was no reply he looked out and there was no one on the crane. Then he heard the footsteps repeated and again he could see nothing to account for them. Officially the explanation was 'vibration' but William Boardman was still dubious, especially when he learned that some years earlier a driver had been killed on that particular crane.

Mayfield railway station is now used as a parcels depot but twenty years ago it was a terminus and shunting yard, a dilapidated old place of crumbling walls, rusty ironwork, cobwebs and broken roofs and platforms, a station that many of the men who worked there believed to be haunted.

As foreman at that time, Fred Jenks knew all about the reputation that the station had; he also knew about the possible cause: two suicides and a fatal accident. A man hanged himself in the indicator box; a former station foreman hanged himself in the gentleman's lavatory; a night workman opened the gate of the baggage hoist thinking the lift was at his level and he fell fifty feet to his death down the shaft. The lift wasn't used after that. Fred Jenks himself heard footsteps that cannot have had a natural origin.

Long after the station was closed for the night and all was dark except for the light in the foreman's office where one man was on duty, heavy and distinct footsteps were heard approaching from the door of another office; they would pass the foreman's office and seem to pause at the window, then the footsteps would continue towards the hoist. There they would cease. Fred Jenks heard these footsteps not once but three times and each time he went to see who was there but he never saw anything, just heard the sound of footsteps reverberating along the deserted platform.

Porter Ted Dyson, tall and tough, said at the time that he had been through a few nasty experiences in his life but he had never come across anything like the strange happenings at Mayfield station. 'You hear the footsteps which don't belong to anybody and a very chilly feeling comes over you. The other night I was sitting here alone when suddenly I felt a prickly feeling up my back and I knew that something was going to happen. Then I heard the footsteps . . .'

Shunter Charlie Movey also related his experiences at the station. The first time was about three o'clock one morning when he was about to go off duty. There was no one else on the station at the time. As he walked towards the office he heard footsteps close behind him. About a fortnight later he heard them again. This time he was near the end of the platform where there was a master switch for all the station lights. 'I grabbed the handle and flooded the whole station with light. I looked everywhere and could see nobody but the footsteps still came towards me, even in the light. They seemed to pass quite close to me and then within seconds they ceased.' In 1977 I was in touch with British Rail, London Midland Region, who told me they could not locate anyone currently employed by British Rail who had any knowledge of 'curious happenings' at Mayfield but, I was told, there were stories of apparitions at Dane Road station – however my enquiries in that direction came to nothing.

A young couple gave up a house of their own and went to live with the wife's parents when they decided that their friendless house in Friendship Street, Gorton, must be haunted. The young couple, Stephen, aged nineteen and his wife Deanna, aged eighteen and their two children, Julie aged two and Andrew four months, needed no great persuasion when Deanna's mother said she had dreamed that young Andrew was in danger. It was the final straw for Stephen who admitted, in October 1972, 'We moved in two years ago and there has always been an atmosphere about the place. Doors have opened by themselves and we have heard noises like people walking up and down the stairs.' Twice Deanna found herself awake in the middle of the night convinced that she had heard a voice ordering her to wake up and she found herself waking up, shouting, 'Go away!'

Mrs Freda Cartwright, Deanna's mother, found the bad atmosphere increasing to such a pitch that she would no longer babysit for her daughter. 'I always felt there was someone else in the house,' she said, 'and latterly nothing would persuade me to go upstairs. Then I had a dream in which I saw my husband's dead father who told us to get the children out of the house in Friendship Street. I went round to them right away.'

At one point Stephen thought about getting a priest to exorcise the house but decided not to bother as nothing would make him live in the house again. His feelings that there was something odd about the house were confirmed when he went back to the house and, although all the doors and windows were secure and there was no sign of any kind of entry, drawers and wardrobe doors were open and clothing was strewn about in one of the bedrooms.

Crumpsall Hospital had a ghost in Ward D3 in 1972, a ghost that seemed to have a passion for lavatory chains, lavatory seats and plastic bowls.

Mr Sidney Hamburger, chairman of the hospital management board stated categorically: 'The plastic basin flew through the air with no apparent cause for the commencement or termination of its journey.' Staff and patients were irritated by the rattling lavatory chains and the banging down of lavatory seats when everyone was trying to get some sleep and no one was anywhere near the swinging chains or the lavatory seats at the crucial times. I have before me a nurse's report that reads:

'There have been several unexplained noises in the sluice room itself:

24.8.72 After closing the sluice door, a Nursing Auxiliary heard a 'bump' and on re-opening the door found a wash bowl gyrating on the floor.

26.8.72 At 1 a.m. an apparition was seen standing underneath the television, and at 6 a.m. there was another 'bump' in the sluice room and another wash bowl was found on the floor.

27.8.72 At 12.40 a.m. a large plastic bowl was flung out of the sluice room across the ward.

Accompanying the above occurrences there was always a 'chilly' atmosphere in the sluice room, perceived by the investigators.

Needless to say, there was no person found in the sluice room.

On Sunday 27th night, Miss Grost and Mr Eastham stayed on the ward between midnight and two o'clock. Nothing was seen.

On Monday 28th night, the Reverend J. Daulman, who had been informed, stayed on the ward from midnight to 1.15 a.m. Nothing was seen, but it was reported to the Rev. J. Daulman that at approx. 11.20 p.m. a lavatory seat was heard to bang and the lavatory chain was found to be swinging vigorously – no one had recently been in the lavatory.'

The Roman Catholic chaplain, Father Joseph Sloane, told me that he was not altogether surprised at the reports since the hospital was a very old one and he had talked with staff and patients who claimed to have seen spectres at bedsides. The Rev. John H. Daulman, the Church of England hospital chaplain, told me that his prayers seemed to have put an end to the mysterious happenings.

The hospital secretary, Mr Brian Colverley, commented, diplomatically: 'I wouldn't like to say that we haven't taken all this seriously but in a hospital of this age and size sounds are difficult to identify in the quiet of the night. The hospital chaplain said a few prayers in the ward because he thought that it might be a useful thing to do and there have been no occurrences since then. We don't know why these things happened but there have been no further incidents.'

A pleasant flat in Northern Drive, Collyhurst, that was the scene of an unsolved murder, was reported to harbour a ghost in 1972, a ghost that was called 'the lady in white'. In March 1970 Mrs Mabel Potter, a fifty-eight-year-old widow, was found battered to death and with throat wounds in the two-bedroomed flat; a man was charged with the crime but was later acquitted and the murder remains officially unsolved.

In November 1972 the two older children of Mrs Martha McLeish, five-year-old Jackie and his three-year-old sister Rhoda were admitted to Booth Hall Hospital, Manchester, suffering 'rather severely' from some form of shock. Mrs McLeish blamed the ghost that she had seen twice before she knew about the murder. 'The children had been constantly crying and talking incoherently and I believe they have seen the ghost that I saw,' she said at the time. 'In the end they were in such a state of nerves that I took them to the hospital.'

The first time Mrs McLeish saw the ghost – which she was convinced was the ghost of the murdered Mrs Potter – was just as she was about to go to sleep one night around midnight. She opened her eyes and saw the figure of a middle-aged woman dressed in white standing looking at her; the figure had auburn hair that was turning grey and as Mrs McLeish watched, paralysed with fear, the form approached her and then disappeared. Mrs McLeish said she saw the same figure five months later. This time she had been to sleep and found herself awake around three o'clock in the morning with the feeling that there was a presence of some kind in the room and then she saw the same figure, but this time it was standing right over her. On each occasion the form was only visible for a few seconds but it was very frightening.

Then, one Sunday night, early in November 1972, after she had put the two children to bed, they both came running out of the bedroom, hysterical and screaming at the tops of their voices that there was 'something' in their room. Mrs McLeish couldn't get much sense out of either Rhoda or Jackie, although the little girl said something that sounded like, 'She was on the cross'; but every night after that both children refused to go to bed in their own room; they were happy enough all day long but became hysterical at bedtime.

Later little Rhoda was able to give a coherent account of the 'lady in white' that she had seen. 'She had long hair, like mummy's,' she said. 'She was on a cross. There was a big band playing. I was very frightened. The bogey woman said to me: "You must wait for me in this room." I said, "Get out of the room." Then she touched me and I ran for my mummy. I don't want to go back there again.' Her brother Jackie, aged five, said, 'She touched my mouth and I was very frightened. I don't want to see her again. I'm glad we're not going back home again.'

Marple, GREATER MANCHESTER

A few miles away from Marple, in a fold of the hills and amid beautiful moorland, an old farmhouse, occupied by Betty Driver of *Coronation Street* fame and her sister Freda, has something like a poltergeist.

One evening in March 1977, Freda and Steuart Kiernander, my wife Joyce and I were entertained at this delightful cottage and heard all about the curious happenings, here and elsewhere. Before they moved into this farmhouse with their boxer dogs, the public house the Drivers ran was the scene of some 'very weird happenings'. In front of dozens of people bottles would rise from their shelves without anyone being near them; bung mallets would hurtle through the air when no one was anywhere near them; and once a cigarette machine that was cemented to the wall came away and fell close to Freda – who seems to attract the supernatural. She had many stories and experiences to relate of strange, unwelcome and very frightening happenings over the years.

Their present home, miles from the bright lights and hurly-burly of city life, is in a part of the country where once scores of Cromwell's men were hanged. An ancient cross marks a long-forgotten battle and all round the hills and fields are haunted. Not very long ago a farmer unearthed a huge circular wheel-like stone with a square hole in the middle; an authority declared that it was a portable gibbet holder. The stone would be rolled to wherever the gallows was needed and erected in the central hole. A nearby lane is now called Gibbs Lane; once it was called Gibbet Lane . . . there is a sombre atmosphere among the quiet hills and dales.

One of the completely inexplicable occurrences experienced by both Betty and Freda Driver are sweet and pleasant perfumes that waft through the cottage, almost as though a posy of old-fashioned flowers was being carried back and forth through the room; less enjoyable are the occasional movements of objects. But as Betty Driver told me: 'I've told Freda I don't mind things moving by themselves and the scent of strange perfume but as soon as I see a soldier hanging from one of our trees – I'm off!'

Low brickwork surrounding a grassy plot of land and vague remains of the once-grand entrance are all that survive of proud Marple Hall, but this mellow spot is still said to be haunted by the headless ghost of Charles I, as was the old Jacobean mansion. Yet it is by no means clear why he should have cause to haunt the vicinity. Marple Hall was owned by Henry Bradshaw whose brother John presided over the council that condemned the King to death but this seems a tenuous reason for the ghostly monarch to haunt Marple Hall – with or without his head.

Mellor Brook, between Blackburn and Preston, LANCASHIRE

Here 'in a secluded dell, on the banks of Mellor Brook' once stood a famous haunted farm. The lonely farm was occupied for generations by a family named Sykes and the property was known – and feared far and wide – by the name of Sykes Lumb Farm.

One of the Sykes who inherited the farm was a thrifty man and he and his wife, by careful living, put by a fair pile of money, to say nothing of the wealth accumulated by his ancestors; yet this little fortune was a matter of concern to them as they grew old for they had no son or daughter of their own and they worried at the thought of it passing to some obscure relative who might squander the money they had saved through many a year. At length they secured the treasure in earthenware jars and buried it deep beneath the roots of a favourite apple tree.

In time the old man died and soon his wife followed him, so suddenly, it is said, that she had no opportunity of disclosing to anyone where the money was hidden and although relatives and friends, knowing of her wealth, searched everywhere they could think of, the treasure was not discovered.

Years later the farm was bought by strangers and the Sykes of Sykes Lumb Farm might have been forgotten and passed into oblivion had it not been for the ghost of old Mrs Sykes. From time to time and usually at dusk, passing neighbours and visiting friends would encounter the form of an old wrinkled woman, bent almost double and dressed in out-of-date clothes, passing silently along the lonely lanes near the old farm. Sometimes the same form would be seen within the precincts of the farm, either disappearing round a farm building or glimpsed for a moment in the old garden among the fruit trees, but always there was something a little frightening about the silent figure with bowed head and crooked stick, a figure that made no sound and so no one ever addressed the strange form. Generations came and went and still the form of the old woman was seen, occasionally within the house itself but more frequently in the garden. Some witnesses described minutely the clothes she wore while others were much too alarmed and ran away from the old farm as fast as their legs would carry them.

At length an occupant of the farm, braver than the rest, a man who had seen the ghostly figure many times, came upon her one day as he was picking apples. He asked her what she wanted and by way of reply she pointed with great emphasis towards some ancient apple trees in the corner of the orchard where the ground had never been disturbed. When the farmer dug in that place he unearthed the treasure that had been buried for so long and as he lifted the heavy jars out of the earth, he caught sight of the phantom old woman, standing a little way off, watching intently. As the last jar was safely recovered, the farmer thought he saw a smile pass over the withered features and when he looked again the figure had gone, nor was it ever seen again.

Middleton, GREATER MANCHESTER

One autumn evening in 1976, accompanied by my wife and Freda and Steuart Kiernander, I called at two interesting old inns, within a stone's throw of each other, and both have the reputation of being haunted.

Middleton is a bustling, commercial place these days but there is a welcome green oasis between the two inns and in the library there it is not difficult to become absorbed in the Middleton of long ago.

The Boar's Head, an inviting and rambling black and white building on the Rochdale road, dates from Tudor times and here we found the 'haunting' somewhat elusive and unsubstantiated – there were stories of vague forms and mysterious lights – but the evidence was slight and unconvincing; whereas across the road a little way the distinctive Ring o' Bells has a ghost story from the past and many reports of strange happenings in recent times. I had first heard of the odd occurrences at this picturesque pub in 1963 from David Cohen, the Investigation Officer of the Manchester Psychical Research Society, when he came to see me at my home.

At that time the licensees were Ernest and Catherine Ryan and on the day that they moved into the Ring o' Bells Catherine distinctly heard *two* sets of footprints pass along the entrance passage of the inn. Only her husband was there at the time, although he too had heard footsteps follow him as he moved things about the inn. During their first night they were both disturbed by the sound of muffled footsteps that seemed to pass along the passage and go into the tap room, sounds that were apparently also heard by the Ryan's pet dog (sleeping that first night in his master's room, situated over the tap room), for the dog ran out of the room and then immediately returned, seemingly excited and frightened by the noises.

Before long one of the phantom forms that has long been said to haunt the Ring o' Bells was seen by Catherine Ryan. At the time she was serving behind the bar and she was in the middle of drawing a drink when she noticed a man in a grey suit, a short, thick-set fellow with a bald head, pass by and make his way into the tap room. A moment later she went to serve him and found no one in the room. There is no door in the room through which the man could have left without being seen from the bar.

The same figure was seen by Tessa Van Brandt, a temporary guest at the inn. She told David Cohen that she was sitting in the tap room very late one night, long after closing time, when suddenly she saw a man in a grey suit coming towards her. Almost as soon as she was aware of the presence, it completely disappeared. She described the atmosphere at the time as 'alive'.

Previous tenants of the inn, Mrs Harlick and Mrs Chapman, also said they had sometimes heard footsteps they could not account for and they also talked of a 'presence' that would occasionally follow people along the passage and into the tap room where it invariably vanished. Mrs Chapman also maintained that several times she and others heard the sounds of movement from the direction of the cellars, as though boxes that were stored there were being shifted or moved about. But always, when anyone went to see what was happening, the noise ceased and there was no sign of anything having been moved. When we were at the Ring o' Bells the landlord took Steuart Kiernander and I down into the cellars where we examined what had once been a fireplace. Obviously the cellars had once been occupied as living quarters. There is certainly a strange atmosphere in this part of the inn.

Other witnesses for the 'grey-suited and bald-headed man' have included a youth who took the figure for a real person and spoke to him. When he received no reply the youth spoke again, in a louder voice; still receiving no answer the young man thought there must be something wrong with the man and he moved towards the figure, whereupon the seemingly solid 'man' vanished. There have also been reports of a mysterious and ghostly woman in grey at the inn.

The two-hundred-year-old hostelry used to house an odd collection of pictures and exhibits that had once belonged to the Middleton Botanical Society who used to meet here: pictures composed of butterfly wings and a stuffed dog are remnants of a strange collection that adds, or once added, a macabre element to the atmosphere and environment of the Ring o' Bells.

The inn has been described as the oldest building in Middleton and there are stories of a Druidic temple having once occupied the site and, much later, tales of monks brewing their beer in the cellars at a time when the building served as a refectory before the Dissolution of the Monasteries. On the other hand, a map of 1767 in the Borough Surveyor's Office does not show any building where the inn now stands, although some old cottages that once stood nearby are clearly shown. The Ordnance Survey map of 1840 shows a building where the inn now stands but does not identify it. Such meagre cartographic evidence must throw some doubt on the Ring o' Bells' best-known ghost, a sad cavalier. That there are stories of secret passages in the vicinity cannot be denied and one is said to have existed in Cromwellian times which ran from the cellars of the inn to the nearby Saxon church.

According to tradition, the cavalier was the son of Lord Stannycliffe of nearby Stannycliffe Hall, a staunch Royalist family at a time when Middleton was something of a Roundhead stronghold. In fact, Cromwell's men used as their headquarters that other haunted pub in Middleton, the neighbouring Boar's Head, while the Royalists met secretly in the Ring o' Bells in the room then used as part of the public house, a room that is now part of the cellar. Actually the 'cellar' they met in is more likely to have belonged to the Church Alehouse, a bawdy tavern of ill repute but certainly helmets, pikes and other articles dating from the Civil War have been found under the cellar floor of the Ring o' Bells.

The introduction of Stannycliffe Hall and the Stannycliffe family into the story is unfortunate. Sir Richard de Stannycliffe seems to have been the last knight of the family; he died *circa* 1300 without male issue and the Hall passed into the possession of the Hopwood family during the 1400s. Incidentally the Hall, which stood at the end of the present Stannycliffe Lane and was finally demolished in about 1834, was also reputed to be haunted.

One day when the cavalier Stannycliffe was in the cellar (so runs the story), he was betrayed to the Roundheads and hurriedly sought to escape by using the secret passage that led to the church, little knowing that Cromwell's men were making use of another underground passage that ran from the Boar's Head to the church. There is the outline of a doorway blocked by heavy stonework in the cellar of the Boar's Head and this is the only tangible evidence of any underground passage in the vicinity. There is sandy subsoil, quite unsuitable for tunnelling; indeed the church has a wooden steeple because, according to a previous rector, the foundations were not sufficiently strong to support a stone one; such evidence as there is must point to the impracticability of underground tunnels hereabouts. However, to return to the story, the cavalier was intercepted, either at the church or nearby, cut down and left for dead. He managed to drag himself back through the passage to the cellar of the Ring o' Bells where he expired and was buried by friends beneath a singular flagstone.

Successive rectors of Middleton have poured scorn on the cavalier story. They say there is no trace in any of the church records of a cavalier being murdered in the church or in the immediate vicinity and local historians aver that there was very little activity in this part of Lancashire during the Civil War. A stone coffin without any inscription on it, containing a male skeleton, was found beneath the nave of the church in 1869 but there is no evidence to connect it with the cavalier story.

Today, above the cellar of the Ring o' Bells, there is a 'snug' or bar-parlour containing 'the cavalier's seat' where some people have felt uncomfortably cold or continually 'have the shivers' when they sit there, although they are warm enough elsewhere in the room; this coldness has been proved to be factual and the area of the seat is often three degrees colder than the cellar itself, but the sceptic points out that this is not surprising in view of the seat being in the direct draught from the passage and two doors.

A former licensee, Mrs Mable (May) Pennystone had no doubt that there were ghostly manifestations at the inn. Although she never saw it, she felt its presence many times and, upstairs in the music room, she often found herself playing a piece of music that she was never in the habit of playing; it was almost as though some force outside herself controlled her fingers and, time after time, she found herself playing 'Greensleeves', a tune that certainly dates back to the sixteenth century and was probably written much earlier, a piece of music that the cavaliers used as a party tune and to which various political ballads were set during the Civil War. Mrs Pennystone always felt the ghost was friendly yet something made her invariably refuse to sleep in the music room. She became very interested in the possibility that the legend of the cavalier could be proved one way or the other by searching for his bones and she hired a local gravedigger, Jack Watson, to raise the flagstones in the cellar and dig into the earth below to see whether he could find anything that would substantiate the story of the ghostly cavalier.

Mrs Pennystone said at the time that if any bones were unearthed she would endeavour to have them buried in the local churchyard. Then, she felt, the cavalier might find rest at last. Unfortunately, in spite of valiant efforts (fortified by frequent pints of beer) and a hole in the cellar floor more than five feet deep, six feet long and three feet wide, nothing but sand was dug out. When I was in the cellar nearly ten years later the landlord had the idea of exploring a part of the old cellar wall that could prove to hide the elusive bones of the cavalier; some of the timbers in the cellar certainly appear to be very old and one part of the wall is excessively thick.

When I asked whether anyone claimed to have seen the ghost cavalier recently I was told that the occupant of an old cottage close to the inn had seen a figure very early one morning. The figure was that of a man dressed like a cavalier, wearing a large, sloppy hat, and he looked very sad. It seems that Mrs Peacock (who was not available when I visited the locality) had time to notice the dark hair hanging in ringlets and she had the impression that the man approaching her, armed with a sword, was crying, although she heard no sound; then suddenly the figure had completely disappeared and she was alone outside the silent Ring o' Bells.

A house in Long Street used to be a gentleman's residence; then it was purchased by a businesswoman who converted it into a shop with a bakehouse at the back and a café in the front. At one time the property had been used as a convent and soon after moving in, the new owner's girls began to say that they frequently heard strange noises and were afraid of being left alone in the place during the evenings; they used to attribute the noises to 'the Mother Superior' and felt that a kindly presence walked about the house but they were certainly scared. Nothing of a tangible nature occurred and the adults did not encourage any mystery being made of the matter, pointing out the possibility of a natural origin for the various noises. But one night the girls' mother was alone in the house when she heard a loud noise that sounded like a load of bricks being dropped. It seemed to come from the direction of the adjoining premises, which were empty at the time, but she said nothing about the matter to anyone.

Some months later, she was giving a lesson on cake decoration in the café to two students when all three heard the same noise: a loud crash exactly as though a load of bricks had been dropped next door. This time a servant came running downstairs saying she had been startled by the noise and wondering what it could be at that time of the evening, it then being about 9.30 p.m. The baker and confectioner thought there must be something wrong next door and she informed the owner of the property, who went through the house from top to bottom but reported that nothing was out of place and that there was nothing to account for the noises that seemed to originate from the house. Both houses were built in about 1794.

The old parish church at Middleton dates from the twelfth century and there is a tradition that it occupies the site of an earlier, wooden church. From time to time communicants and other worshippers have reported seeing the figure of a tall, thin man dressed in a surplice, wandering silently about the church during services and usually disappearing behind one particular pillar. One witness told me that she was in her usual seat in the chancel (she was then in the choir) and was looking towards the back of the pulpit as the curate was preaching when she saw the apparition. She first saw it at the back of the pulpit, a tall, very thin male figure in a surplice; it moved noiselessly behind a pillar and she was surprised that no one took any notice of it and still more surprised when it did not re-appear. Afterwards she mentioned the incident to the curate, who was sympathetic and said he had heard of other people who had seen the same figure but who it was or why it appeared no one seemed to know.

Nantwich, CHESHIRE

Combermere Abbey has a ghost child that may be the fourteen-year-old sister of a previous owner, a child who died suddenly in her sleep.

Over the years many visitors have claimed to encounter this sad-faced wraith and it has been an accepted feature of the Abbey for successive occupants. In 1870 a young lady guest at the house (which stands on the site of an old

Cistercian establishment) was changing for dinner in a bedroom that had once been a nursery. Suddenly she saw a female figure behind her, in the mirror, and turning round saw a girl dressed in an old-fashioned frock with a ruff at the neck, standing looking at her from beside the bed.

For a moment the visitor felt frightened but then she felt that she would like to help her ghostly visitor, if she could, and she walked towards the figure. As she did so the form moved, slowly at first and then faster and faster, round and round the bed! Finally the form seemed to disappear and the young visitor was left wondering whether she had imagined the whole thing, until she related her experience and learned that the young sister of a previous owner had died in her sleep in that room, after she had been chased round and round the bed in fun.

A much older ghost story associated with Combermere tells of the monks removing the bells when the original abbey was dissolved. One bell kept coming adrift and slipped from the boat into the nearby mere; one monk lost his temper and cursed the bell 'by all the fiends of Hell', whereupon the bell broke completely loose and plunged into the depths of the mere, carrying with it the wrathful monk. Neither was ever recovered, although sometimes the sound of a tolling bell is heard, apparently emanating from the depths of the lake and a ghostly monk has been seen between the abbey and the mere.

In February 1977 the present owner, Lady Garnock, told me that there are reputed to be three ghosts – one of which has actually been photographed.

Neston, CHESHIRE

The Quay House at nearby Parkgate, once a prison and then an inn, is reputedly haunted by two ghosts: a little old woman in a red cloak and a tall man wearing a dark cloak. It seems likely that these spectres are as unaware of each other as we are of the association that each may have had with the old building, which has witnessed several changes in its surroundings over the years.

Newton-le-Willows, MERSEYSIDE

Golborne, to the north-east, had a phantom White Lady who has not been seen so frequently since the building of the M6 motorway, although she has even been reported to have flitted across that busy highway.

In 1970 a motor-cyclist said he saw the white figure of a lady float across the road in front of him, causing him to swerve and fall from his machine. Bruised and shaken, he went to the local police station and reported the matter. There he learned that a similar figure had been reported by pedestrians and motorists. Who she is no one knows, but local tradition has it that the White Lady is the victim of a romantic tragedy and she is either looking for her lost love or seeking revenge by causing the deaths of other road-users, one of whom took away the love of her life.

Northwich, CHESHIRE

There is an expanse of shrubland bordering the River Weaver that is haunted by the sounds of spectral horsemen. Colin Lynch tells me that when he lived in Leicester Street this area lay behind his house and although he was unaware of the reputed haunting or the historical significance at the time, an elderly couple living next door told him that they had heard and seen phantom horsemen riding across the shrubland from the direction of Winnington Bridge on several occasions. Knowing these people to be honest and truthful he kept an open mind on the matter.

Some time later one of the local papers published an account of these strange happenings and one person recalled that when he and a friend heard horses approaching them as they were walking across the waste ground one evening, they had stepped to one side to let the horsemen pass, thinking they must be some riders out for a late gallop. When the horsemen passed them they were both astonished to see ghostly figures dressed in Royalist uniforms. Colin Lynch pointed out to me that when one traces the line of retreat from the scene of battle this spot is within half a mile of the conflict that proved to be the last battle of the Civil War. When the Royalist Army was routed they fled across the river in utter confusion and it seems that something of their panic and terror has remained ever since in the area.

A couple of miles north is Marbury Park, an estate now being redeveloped as a country park, and all that remains of haunted Marbury Hall. The ancient manor hall took its name from the Marbury family, who formerly owned it; it became the seat of the Barrymore family in the middle 1700s and they rebuilt it in the 1850s, in the style of a French château. It then descended to the Smith-Barry family who owned the property until the early 1930s. The premises became a country club until the outbreak of the Second World War, when Marbury became a camp for German and Italian prisoners. Later it was taken over by the American Forces; then Imperial Chemical Industries were there for a time, housing many of their workers in the Hall itself and in some barrack-style buildings erected during wartime. During its later years squatters invaded the property and the noble house became a sad sight; it continued to suffer from neglect and vandalism and it was finally demolished in 1968. At that time a long, black and sinister table, with a mirrored top, was stored in a shed; it was this table which was said to have been made to hold the body of the Marbury Lady.

This mysterious personage was embalmed when she died and her body was kept in a coffin in the entrance hall, at the foot of the spiral stairs. But her ghost haunted the house and the next generation thought they would lay the ghost by having the body buried in consecrated ground. So she was buried in the family vault at the church at Great Budworth three miles away. Soon after the funeral service the haunting began again; the ghostly figure was seen, bells in the house rang for no apparent reason and when the disturbances became too troublesome the body of the Marbury Lady was disinterred and returned to Marbury Hall. After things had quietened down again the body in its lead coffin was taken quietly out of the house one night and thrown far out into Budworth Mere. Afterwards her ghost was seen so often that the occupants of the day retrieved the body with great difficulty and buried her beside the wall of the house where, presumably, she still lies.

Legend has it that the real Marbury Lady was a beautiful Egyptian paramour of one of the Barrymores who expressed a wish, as she lay dying, that her body should be embalmed and preserved at Marbury Hall. She had never really been accepted by the majority of the Barrymore family and had lived in almost total seclusion in one part of the enormous mansion but she had grown to love the place. Certain it is that a ghostly 'Lady in White' was reported to walk in the locality for many years; sometimes the spectre was said to be accompanied by a phantom white horse – and this may be the spectre of Marbury Dunne, a famous mare that belonged to the Smith-Barry family whose grave is still in the park. This horse is reputed to have run from London to Marbury between the hours of sunrise and sunset for an enormous wager; indeed it is said that most of the estate was staked on the horse winning the bet. The plucky animal completed the journey with minutes to spare and quenched her thirst so heavily that the shock killed her. The gallant mare was buried by the family with much pomp and ceremony, and presumably she occasionally still visits the scene of her great triumph.

There was also said to be a ghostly 'Lady in Black' at Marbury. Long ago a housekeeper who always dressed in black lived on for some years alone in the Hall and after she was dead her form was reportedly seen walking in the garden at night. In 1959 several people were traced by a local newspaper who had either seen the coffin of the Marbury Lady or had seen one of the ghosts and certainly between 1939 and 1945 many of the prisoners-of-war and others vividly described appearances of the ghosts. A local researcher told me in February 1977: 'There is no doubt that many of the reported sightings were from honest people and not the result of fear or imagination.'

In October 1976, Mr Tom Perrott, Chairman of The Ghost Club, taking part in a meeting devoted to 'A Galaxy of Psychic Anecdotes', revealed the personal experiences of an old family friend, Mrs McLachlan, at Marbury Hall. Tom tells me she is a very down-to-earth type of person and he has no hesitation whatever in personally vouching for her complete integrity. Later he was good enough to write out the story for me.

About the year 1926, Mrs McLachlan qualified as a nurse at the London Hospital; in fact she was one of the first nurses to be trained in the administration of the then new insulin treatment for diabetics. She undertook several cases living in with the families, some of them titled and others very prosperous and well-known people.

She was asked to take over a case at Marbury Hall where she arrived rather late one night. After a meal she was shown to her bedroom and after settling down in bed and sleeping for a short while, she found herself awake and conscious of a sort of mist in the room which materialized into the form of a woman in eighteenth-century costume who gazed at her for a little while and then faded away.

Next morning Mrs McLachlan related her experience of the night to the family at breakfast and they told her that there was a story of haunting associated with the room she was occupying but which they had deliberately refrained from mentioning so that she would not be unduly worried. Having noted her complete composure they said that there was a portrait of their ancestor who was alleged to haunt the room in the portrait gallery and suggested that she might care to accompany them there to see whether she could identify the person she had seen. No sooner had she entered the gallery than, without any hesitation, she pointed to a certain picture and said that was the lady who had been her nocturnal visitor. The family confirmed that her identification was correct.

Oldham, GREATER MANCHESTER

The Radcliffe Arms, as becomes one of the oldest buildings in the area, was once haunted and perhaps still is by the ghost of a man who hanged himself in the cellar. When I was there, in the 1950s, the licensee had many stories to tell of heavy footsteps that clattered across the landing and up the stairs; of glasses that moved in the tap room; of strange creaking noises and stranger sighs and groans that seemed to come from the direction of the cellar or perhaps from the secret passages that are said to lead to nearby Oldham Church; and even the occasional appearances of a harmless phantom, nicknamed 'Ernie', who was seen in the living-room, in the tap room, beside the bar and elsewhere until suddenly, in 1956, the spectre vanished. At the time the landlord, Stan Harrison, and his wife said they were never worried by the ghost and whenever they heard him they used to laugh; such a reaction would surely exorcise any ghost!

In October 1972 a young married couple left their nineteenth-century terraced house in Bradford Street only three months after their wedding because they could no longer stand the antics of their ghosts.

Brian Dunleavy and his wife Bernadette said at the time that they had gone through 'sheer hell' and just 'could not take it any longer'. They moved in with relatives on the other side of Oldham.

Soon after moving in they had noticed odd happenings.

The electricity turned itself on and off, stamping noises were heard in the bedroom, thumping noises seemed to originate from a table in the kitchen and a candle acted very strangely. Their dog, an alsatian, 'lay trembling' in the corner of the room when the noises were heard. Finally Brian reported seeing the forms of two elderly ladies sitting on the settee in the living-room. They were dressed in long, old-fashioned clothes and wore headscarves. When he spoke to them they disappeared.

Brian noticed that at the time he saw the two figures the temperature noticeably dropped and gradually the 'atmosphere of evil' in the house seemed to get more and more powerful until they could stand it no longer.

Two reporters from a local newspaper spent Hallowe'en night of 1972 in the empty house, taking with them camera, tape recorders and thermometers, but their apparatus showed no abnormality and they spent an uneventful and cold night in the quiet little house.

For a time a house in Shaw Road was haunted by the ghost of a former occupant. Two years after the old woman died a phantom female form dressed in a filmy white gown was seen three times by different people and their descriptions were identical and fitted the former elderly resident.

A mill worker, then thirty-nine, Eric Bray, said he was in bed when the form came into the room 'and stood a few feet away from me. I lay watching it for a good three minutes, then it seemed to dissolve and quickly disappeared. The old woman was dressed in a long white gown that looked more like mist than anything else. She didn't speak . . . I don't know what I would have done if she had!'

After a neighbour saw the same figure and also watched a table move by itself across the floor, a medium was called to the house and she immediately described the same figure. After a seance had been held in the house the ghost was not seen again.

Plumley, near Knutsford, CHESHIRE

Tabley Old Hall, now a farm, is said to be haunted by the ghosts of a man and a woman whose forms have sometimes been reported leaning over the old balustrade. The ghosts are thought to be those of a jealous husband who was killed in a duel, and his wife who committed suicide. To avoid a scandal their bodies were reputedly walled up inside the house and their ghosts are doomed to haunt the house they knew in happier times until their bodies are found and buried in consecrated ground.

Radcliffe, near Bury, GREATER MANCHESTER

In Railway Street, late in 1972, a building was demolished that dated back to 1849. The premises had once been the Commercial Hotel but it was later, when it had served as a telephone exchange, that strange happenings were reported.

One day in 1951 the engineer in charge, Jack Smethurst, noticed a sudden drop in temperature and saw a hazy and indistinct shape rise from the floor and grow until it reached the ceiling, where it disappeared. He said at the time: 'Although I don't believe in ghosts as such, I do believe there was something there that could not be explained.' There were reports that the same phenomenon was witnessed by five other people on different occasions, right up to 1972 when two schoolboys, Kevin Higgins and Robert Schofield, on their way home from school decided to have a look at the old building. Afterwards they said they saw a 'sort of grey mist' that frightened them. It was only later that they heard about the 'ghost mist' that was long reputed to haunt the place.

Tradition has it that the ghostly form was associated with a sailor who was knifed to death in the cellar, or with a landlord of the Commercial Hotel who was murdered. A portrait of a bearded man, engraved on a window and thought to represent the murdered landlord, was removed by a local historical society when the property was demolished and is now preserved in the local library.

Ribchester, LANCASHIRE

A mile south, on the other side of the River Ribble, stands Osbaldeston Hall, now part of a farm and mostly Elizabethan but once the thirteenth-century home of the Osbaldeston family, who lived here for more than seven hundred years. During the turbulent sixteenth century the quick-tempered Thomas Osbaldeston is said to have killed his brother-in-law in a duel at the Hall and thereafter the room where the duel took place was haunted both physically and psychically, for the dark bloodstains on the floorboards could never be erased and from time to time residents and visitors complained of heart-rending moans and groans and gasps, as from a dying man; less frequently a phantom form was reported to glide about the Hall, its arms upraised to reveal blood pouring from a mortal wound in the chest.

The Osbaldeston family have been gone from here for more than two hundred years now but still the story of the restless victim lingers on and when I was there in March 1977 the old house seemed to exude an atmosphere of unwelcome and brooding malevolence.

Rivington, LANCASHIRE

The village of Rivington spans the Rivington Reservoir that supplies the Liverpool area with water. South of Headless Cross, the vicinity of Anderton has been reputed to be haunted since time immemorial by the figure of a monk who disappeared mysteriously, a ghost that is said to be that of a Father Bennet who sought to hide some church valuables at the time of the Dissolution of the Monasteries. He was thought to have entered an underground tunnel leading to the monastery and was never seen again.

In October 1968 a seventy-five-year-old widower, Mr James Wilkinson of Winter Street, Horwich, said he believed the ghost was in fact that of his great-uncle, a gamekeeper who looked and sought in vain for three milkmaids who were not what they seemed to be.

James Wilkinson's great-uncle was named Joe Hill and he was head gamekeeper at Anderton Hall, demolished in 1930. 'One night,' James Wilkinson relates, 'about a hundred years ago, my mother, then a young girl, went to Joe's lonely cottage to take him some food. He was out but nearby she found the body of his retriever dog which had been killed by about twenty wounds from a pitchfork. My mother used to tell me that she saw three poachers wearing milkmaids' bonnets hurrying away from the scene of the crime. Sometimes, I think, Joe comes back to try and catch the men who killed his dog.'

The ruins of Rivington Castle have long been reputed to be haunted by an unknown spectre and in 1967 five Horwich workmen watched, for something like two hours, a white figure moving around the castle grounds. It was early in the morning at about 5.30 a.m. when Mr Richard Dabbs was removing some pipes from a kiln that he noticed a glistening white shape on the highest point of the castle ruins. It reminded him of a mirror reflecting the sun but later when the sun had risen he could make out an indistinct white shape. He thought to himself that there was unlikely to be anyone up there at that time in the morning so he stopped to watch. The shape moved a little to one side and then back again after about ten minutes. Richard went back and told his workmates what he had seen but they didn't really believe him and he forgot about the matter for half an hour or so.

Then one of his fellow workers went outside for something and he came running back saying he too had seen something white moving about the ruins. All four of the men then went outside and saw the white shape moving about the castle grounds, in and out of the bushes, at the foot of the ruins. They continued to watch and it seemed as though the mysterious white figure was keeping a lookout. It followed the same track repeatedly, going back and forth from the bottom of the castle to the top and then back again; sometimes it disappeared behind bushes but it always reappeared, vividly white against the grey stones of the castle.

Then, at about 7.30 a.m., it disappeared behind some bushes and was not seen again, nor did the men see it on subsequent mornings but they worked out that it must have been almost ten feet in height to be so clearly visible from where they were standing, nearly three miles away.

Rochdale, GREATER MANCHESTER

The old graveyard of St Mary's is reputed to be haunted by the ghost of an unidentified man, a figure that drifts across the area after dark. It used to pass through a wall into the market and across the market itself where it vanished; but now the whole area has been rebuilt. The same place has long been said to be haunted by a spectral rabbit.

The Rev. Alan Shone has been good enough to provide me with information on these apparitions although he is careful to make the point that he has been at St Mary's since 1945 and has not yet seen the rabbit. When he first went to Rochdale he came across many people who spoke about the unusual phantom but no one who had actually seen it. He tells me the tale goes back to the middle of the eighteenth century when the church was founded and the graveyard opened. Locally the graveyard was known as 'The Baum', from an old Lancashire term for a certain medicinal herb that grew there and from which the local apothecaries mixed their nostrums. So the ghost rabbit has always been known as 'The Baum Rabbit' to local people.

During the years that he lived at the Old Rectory beside the church, where he lived until he moved into the new Vicarage in April 1976, the rector stopped many times in the lane that runs past the graveyard at night, waiting in the hope of seeing one or the other of the reputed ghosts but he never saw either.

When the old graveyard was sold to the local corporation for a new road in 1974, it had to be cleared and it was dug out twenty feet deep and something like three hundred bodies were removed, all of them eighteenth century. The rector was there the whole time that the men were working, partly because he felt it was his duty as incumbent and partly because he wanted to see whether there were any rabbit burrows. It was, as he put it, 'a grisly experience' but no rabbit warrens whatever were encountered. In these circumstances Mr Shone concluded that whatever the explanation for the 'Baum Rabbit', it seems unlikely to have been a real live rabbit; it could possibly have been a pet rabbit that had escaped or a cat or even a small dog. In actual fact the rector tells me he only once saw a rabbit there in thirty years but he is quite sure it was a real flesh and blood animal and no apparition – but where it came from and where it went he never discovered and he never saw it again.

A hundred years ago, in a *Guide to Rochdale*, William Robertson devoted a chapter to the Baum Chapel (as St Mary's was once called) and the 'Baum Rabbit'. He says: 'Whether any of the present generation have seen the ghostly rodent, we will not undertake to say. In former days, or rather nights, it used to revisit the chapel yard. It was a rabbit of robust and lively habits and was plump and well nourished, as if the churchyard herbage agreed with it. It was always beautifully clean, and was even said to be whiter than snow. It used to be seen in various attitudes, sometimes standing on its hind-quarters, after the manner of rabbits, demurely brushing its whiskers.

'Its aspect was usually somewhat serious, although at times

it had a comical twist of countenance. It has also been observed delving into the churchyard mould with great determination, as if in search of hidden treasure. But no one that we have heard of ever came to close quarters with it. The slightest attempt to hold a parley with the mysterious quadruped was utterly useless; for, being exquisitely sensitive to the slightest sound, it invariably disappeared into thin air when intruded upon, and thus eluded the investigations of the earnest enquirer after truth. Strange to say, it was apparently much pleased with the love (but not lovely) music of the cat tribe, to which it listened with mute attention. Clearly, the rabbit was invulnerable to the nocturnal sportsman's small-shot, and even air guns, it is alleged, had no effect on it. After a discharge from any deadly weapon, it used to reappear with the greatest equanimity, and frisk about as if to encourage its assailants to further effort in the same direction. Some people said the smell of gunpowder was as delicious to it as a pinch of snuff to an old woman. It was generally admitted that it was a rabbit of a ghostly or supernatural character. The story runs that hundreds of years before the erection of the "Baum Chapel" a deed of horror was committed within the precincts haunted by this extraordinary rabbit; but, unfortunately, authentic particulars of that dark transaction have never been obtained, and we are, therefore, unable to gratify the remarkable curiosity of the reader on the subject.

'It is agreed on all hands that, as a rabbit, it was remarkably well behaved, and never, so far as could be ascertained, committed any serious wrong. Its chief object seemed to be to scare folks a bit, and it gave no token of being influenced by any diabolical agency. Doomed to haunt the churchyard for a certain term, it would seem, from recent experience, that it has performed its allotted task, for very little is heard in our day of the surprising "Baum Rabbit", which used to perplex the natives and fright them from their propriety. It is with reference to this curious animal that an ancient local poet, in an angry mood, wrote the following verses. He had to pass through the churchyard every night on his way home, and was, to say the least of it, of a very nervous temperament.

> Confound that rabbit!
> I wish some chap would grab it,
> And stop its nightly habit;
>   Confound that rabbit!
>
> Confound its head and eyes!
> Confound its legs and thighs!
> Confound it otherwise!
>   Confound that rabbit!
>
> Dogs, rush out and squeeze him!
> Worry, toss, and tease him!
> That is, if you can seize him.
>   Confound that rabbit!

Mr Shone tells me that one of his congregation, a gentleman in his middle seventies, told him that it was a long time since anyone claimed to have seen the phantom rabbit and perhaps the haunting, if haunting it was, has ceased.

A man in knee-breeches has been known to walk from the graveyard towards the river. Mr Shone's son, a policeman, was the first person to inform the rector of this apparition. Several of his colleagues on night duty having seen it, some of them conceived it their duty to accost it, without success. Now the old graveyard and the market have gone, and even the Lordburn stream has been diverted, yet still there are occasional sightings of a strange and silent figure that seems to float above the surface of the ground as if unaware of its surroundings.

Before it was demolished, the Vavasour Hotel was the scene of strange happenings, according to the late David Cohen, Investigation Officer for the Manchester Psychical Research Society. He told me that he visited the establishment about four months after Mr and Mrs Donald Cash had taken charge of the hotel.

Some of their customers had reported odd occurrences but the first incident witnessed by Mr and Mrs Cash concerned the door between the living quarters and the bar; quite simply it repeatedly opened and closed by itself. David Cohen was not unduly impressed by this 'phenomenon' since, although the door was fitted with a strong return spring, he discovered that when certain upstairs doors were open a strong draught was created which could account for the movement of this particular door.

Mr Edward Fleming, the barman, related that when he had gone down into the hotel cellar, a couple of weeks after the new landlord had moved in, he had felt a presence close behind him. It was a very strong impression and at first he thought Donald Cash had followed him down the steps but on turning round, he discovered that he was alone.

About a week later Mrs Cash was serving a customer, assisted by Mrs Alice Northover. The cash register was faulty and was therefore temporarily left open. Suddenly both women heard the sound of the cash register drawer closing and they both saw it move as they watched.

During the course of an all-night visit in November 1963, David Cohen and his fellow investigators reported a quiet and uneventful night.

The Baron family of Kirkholt were disturbed night after night in 1958 for several weeks when loud crashes and banging noises echoed through their house. At first they looked at each other and blamed the neighbours; then they noticed that the noises only began after their nine-year-old daughter, Janet, had gone to bed – until one night the little girl went to bed an hour later than her usual time and the noises started while she was still downstairs.

The Barons sent for the police; the police informed the Waterworks Department and their inspector, carrying out a routine check on the plumbing, heard the noises himself. He left the house in something of a hurry, saying as he went, 'Your water system is all right.'

The next development took place when a caller at the house knocked on the front door and everyone heard a knock in reply from inside the house. This was repeated a number of times; each time the unexplained knocks seemed to come from the floor in the vicinity of Janet's bedroom door. They experimented time and time again and each time anyone tapped anywhere in the house, no matter how lightly, an answering knock came from the child's bedroom door. It 'performed' for the reporter of a local newspaper, then for the family doctor, Dr Donald Glen; and for the local vicar, the Reverend W. H. Vanstone, who decided that the family had a poltergeist.

An electronics engineer was consulted and he thought the knocking might be either the result of some accidental arrangement of the electrical supply, a freak of resonance within the walls, or something to do with the water supply. A psychiatrist thought it might be something to do with the little girl – although he thought this unlikely due to her age – or perhaps the electricity, the walls or the gas supply. And still the knocks continued to sound before they grew weaker and then ceased.

Rostherne, CHESHIRE

Rostherne Mere, three miles south-west of Altrincham, is reputed to be haunted by the sound of a ringing bell each Easter morning.

Many years ago the village church at Rostherne was badly in need of repair, especially the belfry, which had to be rebuilt before it was safe to hang the new bells. Then, when everyone thought all was well, the largest bell broke away from its mooring ropes and rolled down the hill to the mere. Twice the bell was dragged back up to the church and twice it broke loose, until one of the local men, tired of the whole affair, gave the offending bell a kick and told it to go to the Devil. No sooner were the words out of his mouth than the great bell lurched backwards on to the speaker, killing him outright, and then it broke loose again and rolled far into the mere where it disappeared with fearsome bubbling sounds and muffled chimes.

The Rostherne Mere is said to be bottomless and the bell was never recovered but once a year it is said a disturbance of the water can be seen, far out in the centre of the mere, and the bell appears above the surface, breaking the water with a splash. A few chimes sound across the still lake and then the bell descends back into the deepness of the mere for another twelve months.

Rufford, LANCASHIRE

Rufford Old Hall, ancient seat of the Hesketh family, has a 'Grey Lady' ghost that haunts the house and grounds. Her form, clear and solid-looking, but throwing no shadow, has been seen near the house and in the drive that leads to the church; she has also been seen in a room on the ground floor – apparently enjoying a piano recital given by a mere mortal!

The ghost is commonly believed to be a former Lady of Rufford who waits for ever for her husband, or lover, to return from some forgotten escapade.

In 1948 a local museum curator is reported to have located evidence that the Grey Lady was a lonely young woman whose husband was summoned to a Scottish war in the middle of their wedding celebrations. Some time later an old warrior, passing through the village on his return from the same skirmish, gave her the news that her husband was on his way home. Accordingly a great feast was prepared in his honour and the whole village and many of the surrounding local people gathered at the Hall; but the hours passed and then the days and the Lord of Rufford failed to arrive. The young bride vowed that she would wear her wedding gown until he did come, saying, 'I know he will return tomorrow'. Tomorrow came and went, the distressed girl refused her food, she slowly lost her strength and on her deathbed declared that her spirit would wait on at the Hall until her beloved did return, forever if necessary.

At one time a custodian of this National Trust property declared: 'I have known the building intimately all my life and I have seen the Grey Lady.' An authority on Rufford and its history stated: 'I never saw the Grey Lady myself although I was present when she was reported to have walked and I have known many people who have seen her.'

When the late Lord Hesketh gave the Hall to the Trust in 1936, his family had been at Rufford since the thirteenth century, so presumably the Grey Lady must be a Hesketh. Yet when, thanks to the kind co-operation of the present curator, Mr H. B. Ratcliffe, the Hall was specially opened for my wife and I in March 1977, we were told of an alleged appearance by the ghost of Queen Elizabeth I in the dining-room some years ago.

Runcorn, CHESHIRE

At the end of August 1952 I began to receive reports of a very curious and persistent outbreak of poltergeist activity at No. 1 Byron Street; I was still receiving news of disturbances there in 1956, and by that time the case had become famous as 'the Runcorn Poltergeist'.

The majority of the manifestations took place between August and October 1952 and while some authors and investigators have described the case as constituting the best attested recent story of poltergeist phenomena in England, others treated the whole matter with extreme scepticism; such is the fate of all poltergeists. My own opinion lies somewhere between these two extremes.

The first reports told of furniture moving by itself in a bedroom and of books being dashed to the floor in the darkness of the night. There were many witnesses to these happenings including policemen and one sergeant stated that a dressing-table had moved in his presence as he ascertained from marks on the floor, but nobody saw anything because it all happened in the dark and 'as there was no material evidence to show how it became moved, it ceased to be a matter for the police.'

The house was occupied at the time by Mr Samuel Jones (aged sixty-eight), his widowed daughter-in-law, Mrs Lucy Jones, his grandchildren John and Eileen Glynn (aged sixteen and eight respectively) and a middle-aged spinster Miss Ellen Whittle, who was unfortunate enough to fall into a quarry on 22 October 1952, and died in hospital the following day.

After four nights of almost unceasing disturbances, noises and the sudden movement of objects, the family were on the brink of leaving the house when a spiritualist medium spent three hours there and the strange happenings ceased. The medium gave an astonishingly accurate description of John Glynn's father, who had died a few months previously, and whose spirit, the medium said, was standing by the dressing-table in the haunted room. The medium maintained that the deceased Mr Glynn's spirit was earthbound and had somehow picked up an evil poltergeist connection responsible for the more violent phenomena. The dead man was known to have been a heavy smoker and during the seances strong smells of tobacco smoke were reported, although no one in the house was smoking at the time and no one had smoked in the room prior to the seance. 'There were times,' said Mrs Lucy Jones, 'when as many as a dozen people were in the house. Various tests were made and everybody who has been in the bedroom when the furniture moved was convinced that the thing was inexplicable.'

Mr Frank Watson, who lived opposite, said he had not believed the stories until he spent several hours at the 'haunted house' himself. 'When I was there, only three of us were in the bedroom. The other two were John Berry from Picow Street and John Glynn. We turned off the light and I stood near the door with my hand on the switch. We were quiet for a few minutes. Without any prior warning I heard the dressing-table being moved and at once I switched on the light. It had been shifted a few inches. We pushed it back and again turned off the lights. Soon afterwards the noise returned and quickly the light was turned on once more. This time the dressing-table had been carried a little further. We pushed it back again and at the same time put a tumbler on the edge of the dressing-table. It was certain to fall if that piece of furniture was given a jerk. We decided to keep the light off a little longer to see how far the dressing-table could be moved. I still had my hand on the switch when the noise started again but I still refrained from switching on the light; however, some people were in the next room and they switched on their light which was reflected into our room. The noise stopped immediately and as I turned on our light I noticed that the dressing-table had moved more than a foot, and the tumbler was still balanced on the edge. I would not have cared to sleep in that bedroom on my own!' Mr Watson was struck by the fact that the dressing-table was always swung out from one end, exactly as it would have been by a man commencing to move a heavy object. The noise at this time sounded like drawers being opened and closed again quickly. 'It was the most terrible week I have ever known,' Mrs Lucy Jones said at the time. 'Two Bibles, a picture book, a tin of ointment and a table cover were thrown violently to different parts of the room. We were all terrified nearly out of our wits and young John was a wreck.'

The disturbances returned a couple of days later when unexplained noises emanated from the dressing-table, a clock and other articles were thrown across the bedroom in the presence of independent witnesses and now the phenomena began to take place with the light on and sometimes when no one was in the room. Then, following a visit by a Roman Catholic priest, the strange happenings again ceased for sixteen days and nights, but then began again, seemingly with renewed strength and violence. In the presence of seven independent observers, including newspaper reporters and a psychic investigator, the force proceeded to smash furniture and bombard the watchers with books, drawers and small articles for six hours on end. Even John Glynn himself was thrown about the room. The bed, with three men seated on it, was suddenly moved; a heavy chest danced, the dressing-table rocked and persistent raps on the door and windows all combined to produce a crescendo of sound that made speech impossible. Already the crowds of sightseers who nightly gathered outside the house caused sceptical neighbours to suggest that a light be left on in the house all night but since this would, in all probability, keep the ghosts at bay, it would also do away with the publicity – which some members of the household now seemed to be enjoying.

The Rev. W. H. Stevens, a member of the Society for Psychical Research, then came on the scene and after visiting the house and hearing about the disturbances first-hand suggested that there was 'no evidence that the trouble had a spiritualistic or other-world influence; it centred around a boy of about seventeen and was caused by an excessive vitality in young people which could be released through a stratum of the unconscious mind.'

By the time October had arrived it was noticed that Sunday nights usually produced the most violent phenomena and by then it was claimed that objects were thrown about the house and raps and taps were heard when John Glynn, generally considered to be the nexus of the poltergeist, was not even in the house. On one occasion when he was in the house a book hit John in the corner of his left eye and bruised the skin so that his eye was discoloured for more than twenty-four hours. By now the bedroom was a shambles; the furniture was smashed and the walls chipped to the brickwork in places by flying objects; even the ceiling of the room beneath was badly cracked and much of the plaster had come away. All this was apparently caused by a strange force that suddenly made itself felt in the house. Heavy furniture was broken to matchwood, witnesses were beaten by pieces of wood torn from the furniture, people were pulled and thrown about and bombarded with everything in the room that could be thrown.

The BBC then showed an interest in the proceedings and they set about recording an eye-witness account of the activities; a programme was duly recorded but, typically, the 'poltergeist' was inactive at the time. Two days later, a Sunday, the 'geist' returned and five books were thrown across the bedroom, John Glynn being hit four times out of the five!

By early November only slight activity was being reported although for a while 'something' seemed to follow John when he moved to live with his mother in Stenhills Crescent. A month later a visitor to Byron Street said he saw one of the occupants throw a book from the bed, after banging it against the wall – and so the Runcorn poltergeist case seemed to come full circle and conformed with the vast majority of such cases, beginning with easily explained happenings, gradually becoming more puzzling and more violent and apparently localized and associated with a teenager before finally there are suspicions of conscious fraud and then the case slips into oblivion. But the Runcorn poltergeist was a complex affair and years after the first raps were reported other curious happenings were being connected with the case. Let me reveal some of the private information given to me at the time by the Rev. W. H. Stevens who investigated the case on the spot on my behalf.

He told me that John Glynn was a good-natured lad of average intelligence and more than willing to submit to any test, even to the tying of his hands and feet. It is unfortunate that, by the time Mr Stevens had won the confidence of the family and was able to impose any restrictions and take any liberties and just when I was about to organize and conduct experiments under controlled conditions with a few picked investigators, the activities petered out.

Mr Stevens did talk to the police sergeant who carried out some sort of investigation soon after the disturbances started and he said John Glynn was in a state of nervous collapse, but he added, 'I tried everything known to me and believe me the boy was not responsible; why, I am not strong enough to make the dressing-table dance about as it did and I'm sure John Glynn couldn't do it.' There were several assertions that the bedroom or part of it was suddenly cold on occasions but Mr Stevens told me that his thermometers registered no abnormality.

During the course of a visit to the house in November Mr Stevens took with him three reporters and two local men, a Mr Davies and a publican from Kingsley. Nothing happened and eventually all the visitors gathered in a room opposite the 'haunted' bedroom where John Glynn and his friend John Berry occupied the double bed and Sam Jones lay in a single bed. They had all been in bed about three hours when a noise was heard and the publican and a reporter stole quietly to the door of the room to see what was happening. The publican declared that in the light of his torch he saw Sam Jones bang a book three times on the wall and then throw it across the room. The reporter beside him confirmed the throwing of the book. The visiting party went downstairs to discuss the matter and it was decided not to demand an immediate explanation. Later when Mr Sam Jones was questioned on the matter he said he scarcely remembered the incident but he might have thrown a book off the bed in annoyance. On the other hand most of the reported happenings took place when the grandfather, Mr Sam Jones, was not present. Mr Stevens believed, after spending eleven nights in the house, that the early occurrences possessed a genuine element but later, when the affair was petering out, some efforts were made to keep it going.

A few months later Mr Stevens was in touch with me again on the subject: 'Please find enclosed a further Report on the Runcorn Case . . . I wonder what you will make of it. At one time I thought I had the Runcorn affair "in the bag" but this Crowther story has upset my ideas. I came across an accountant who visits the Crowthers. He told me the story is perfectly true and in their distress they had asked his advice . . . Mr Crowther is having no more pigs; he is growing mushrooms instead.'

During the course of this report Mr Stevens confirmed that Mr and Mrs Crowther had endured some distressing experiences on their farm at Runcorn, which had some connection with the poltergeist haunting at Byron Street. It seemed that Sam Jones was a part-time worker on the farm and on 10 August (a week before the Byron Street disturbances began), a pig mysteriously died. No special significance was attached to this incident but before the end of the week three more pigs were dead. By the end of a fortnight all fifty-three pedigree pigs had died. No less than five veterinary surgeons were called in but none could give any explanation for the deaths; entrails of the animals were sent for examination but the cause of death remained a mystery.

Two days after the loss of the last pig Mr Harold Crowther was astonished to see a large black cloud, about seven feet in height, moving about the yard. It was a shapeless mass except for two prongs sticking out at the back. It moved along the yard towards him, then turned to the left and disappeared in the direction of the empty pigstys. He said nothing about this to anyone, afraid that people would say he had imagined it. Two days later his wife told him she had seen a strange cloud in the yard. Whether the farm animals saw anything or not he could not say but he found some of the stock fighting for no apparent reason and one cow began to bellow loudly and seemed to be in a state of intense fear, its eyes bulging, the hair on its back standing on end and covered in perspiration. From that day the cow gave no more milk.

Curious noises now began to be heard in the kitchen of the farmhouse; drawers in a desk rattled by themselves and jam pots on shelves shuddered and overturned. On Sam Jones's invitation, Harold Crowther visited the 'haunted house' in Byron Street and there saw the same black cloud with its two prongs hovering over the bed where John Glynn lay. Harold Crowther returned to his farm and never went to the house in Byron Street again.

Early in December, after the Byron Street disturbances had virtually ceased, Harold Crowther saw the cloud yet again – this time actually within the kitchen of his home. Determined to find out what it was, he brushed by it to switch on the light. As he did so the two prongs touched him on the left side of his throat; they felt solid, like blunt sticks. By the time the light was switched on the cloud had disappeared. The farmhouse dates from the fifteenth century and the Crowthers had their nine-year-old son living there with them.

A week later when Harold Crowther opened the door of a large shed in which two dogs slept, a spaniel and a sheep dog, the dogs rushed out excitedly as was their habit; turning, Harold Crowther saw the cloud on his left again. It seemed to be smaller and lighter in colour and density. It moved along the ground, rose up into the air and disappeared. The dogs saw it too, they barked and jumped up at it. This was the last time the cloud was seen and the end of disturbances at the farm and, for all practical purposes, at Byron Street. The Runcorn poltergeist had run its course.

St Helens, MERSEYSIDE

Croppers Hill, on the Liverpool road, used to be called Combshop Brow, after a cottage with a large garden that stood near the top of the hill and was occupied for many years by an old comb-maker, famous throughout the area for his workmanship. Down at the bottom of the hill there used to be a brick building that was the scene of a curious occurrence which has never been satisfactorily explained.

The upper stories of this building were used as offices and showrooms while the lower part of the premises were given over to the manufacture of flint glass. For many years there were stories of mysterious happenings and even appearances of inexplicable figures in the property but it was on a Wednesday afternoon, just over a hundred years ago, at three o'clock precisely that the affair came to a head.

At that hour on a Wednesday in September 1875, an industrious, loyal and reliable glass engraver was working away quietly when suddenly a shower of stones came crashing through the front window of the building. Rushing out to ascertain the cause of this unprovoked disturbance he was astonished to find a crowd of people in the roadway below throwing stones at the building! Dozens of people asserted that they had seen a ghost at the window and they wanted to see whether it could withstand a hail of stones! In vain the manager and staff tried to placate the people and get them to move away; instead more and more people arrived at the scene and eventually the police had to clear the street.

For days afterwards passers-by and local people and visitors asserted that the place was haunted and that they could see a ghostly face at the window. By now nearly every pane of glass in the building had been smashed but still the crowds collected. Boards were fixed up to protect the property and gradually the excitement died down and the affair passed into local history. Work at the factory was brought to an abrupt end and the premises were locked and boarded up. For years afterwards the broken and shuttered windows remained witness to the destruction allegedly caused by the appearance of a ghost; even today the area is reputed to be haunted.

The locality of Crank, a couple of miles north of St Helens, has long been reputed to be the haunt of a ghostly white rabbit. This strange apparition, described as being 'large and having lopping ears' was greatly feared a hundred years ago for people who said they had seen the ghost rabbit died shortly afterwards and others experienced great calamities.

It seems that the White Rabbit of Crank was in the habit of suddenly appearing in front of travellers and hopping alongside them for a while. One witness said he had just passed the inn at Crank in his horse-drawn cart when he saw the rabbit cross the road and wait for him to approach. Instead he hurriedly tied his horse to a tree and ran back over fields and ditches to the farm which he had left. He refused to set foot on that stretch of road again that day and the farmer himself had to go and fetch the horse and cart.

The legend that is said to account for the ghostly white rabbit goes back to the days of James I when superstition was rife and Matthew Hopkins, the 'witchfinder general', was actively engaged in hunting out his victims. At this time there lived at Crank an old woman who was regarded with something like awe by the whole neighbourhood, for she was of foreign extraction and lived a solitary existence, her only companion being her little grand-daughter, named Jenny, whose dearest possession was a pet white rabbit. The old woman was knowledgeable about herbs and their healing powers and, since she was also thought to have studied the occult arts, this resulted in her being regarded locally as a witch.

One of the local farmers was named Pullen; he was a small, dark and repulsive bachelor who was reputed to be something of a miser and when he found that he was suffering from a wasting disease that grew worse as the months passed, he resorted to obtaining some herbal concoctions from Jenny's grandmother. Still there was no improvement in his condition; in fact his health seemed to be deteriorating more quickly and he became convinced that the 'old witch' was poisoning him. He therefore resolved to break the spell by 'drawing blood' from old 'Mother Pope', a recognized method of obtaining relief in such circumstances.

Pullen enlisted the help of a local character named Dick Piers, a worthless rogue who had been drummed out of the army and made a living from poaching and other nefarious activities. Together, their faces blackened and thoroughly disguised, they set out one dark night for the old woman's cottage. All was quiet and still. They burst in, found the old woman in bed, dragged her halfway across the floor of the room and made a clean cut in her arm from which the blood flowed freely. Their mission accomplished, they prepared to leave the terrified old woman when Jenny, half-asleep and full of terror, entered the room clutching her pet rabbit in her arms. Seeing the two men who had attacked her grandmother and fearful for her own safety, she sped down the stairs and ran as fast as she could out into the night.

Fearing that she would alarm the neighbourhood and expose them for what they were, Pullen and Piers dashed after her. They thought they saw her disappearing over a hill and gave chase. When they were near the top of the hill Jenny's rabbit hopped out of a hedge and approached them. With an oath Piers kicked the defenceless creature high into the air and when it fell at his feet, Pullen continued the ill-treatment until the dead and battered body landed in a ditch. But of Jenny they could find no trace and at length they made their way home, hoping that all would be well.

Next morning the body of little Jenny was found, cold and stiff, her feet torn and her head cut where she had fallen. Old Mother Pope recovered from her ordeal but could give no clue as to her assailants. Poor Jenny was buried and Mother Pope soon left her cottage for a more congenial locality. The whole affair might have been forgotten had it not been for the rabbit.

Dick Piers continued to pursue his wild ways and a month or so after Jenny's funeral he was making his way home across some fields when suddenly he saw, to his horror and amazement, Jenny's rabbit hopping leisurely across the field towards him! There was no mistaking the animal; there was not another like it with its enormous white lopped ears and great pink eyes . . . after a second look, he turned about and ran home another way as fast as he could. But Piers was a doomed man. The white rabbit haunted his imagination and it seemed forever on his mind. After a few weeks he suddenly made a full confession of his share in the attack on Mother Pope at the local inn and then rushed out. Next morning his body was found at the bottom of a quarry.

Pullen denied all knowledge of the affair and he lived on, becoming more and more morose and solitary, alone with his memory and his conscience. His health continued to deteriorate.

One evening he chanced to find himself in the vicinity of Mother Pope's deserted cottage. With a sigh of regret that, in spite of all he had done, the spell that he believed had been put on him had not been broken, he turned away and set off for home. He had taken hardly a dozen steps when he discovered that a large white rabbit was keeping him company and a thrill of terror ran through him as he recognized the animal. He ran, and the rabbit ran too, he turned and the rabbit turned also, he stopped and the rabbit stopped too. In desperation he raced over dark fields, round and round, until he collapsed from exhaustion. He was found and cared for but the fright and the exposure had completed the work of the disease he had and he died a week later.

Some people say that with the coming of the railway line the ghostly rabbit disappeared; other local people insist that the White Rabbit of Crank is still seen occasionally on dark nights and that those who see it always regret that they do so.

Sale, GREATER MANCHESTER

Towards the end of 1976 Freda and Steuart Kiernander showed me the house in Sale once occupied by actress Pat Phoenix. The old Georgian house looked solid and comfortable but when she lived there it housed a ghost; 'a friendly soul of whom I really became quite fond,' Pat Phoenix told me.

It all began one night when she was sitting down in the lounge, resting. Suddenly she saw the hackles rise on her corgi dog and he began to pace up and down one wall, whining. Then she saw the figure of an old lady carrying a soup bowl walk past the door. As soon as she recovered from her surprise Miss Phoenix searched the whole house but there was no one anywhere; however she did notice a very cold spot in one of the rooms. 'Strangely,' she said, 'I wasn't frightened. I just thought to myself – Pat, you are seeing an apparition. It didn't bother me at all.'

She saw the same figure several times afterwards. There always seemed to be a bump or thump from somewhere in the upper part of the house before the figure was seen – usually between 9.30 and 10 o'clock in the evening. 'Of course people were sceptical when I spoke about it, but several other people have also seen the same figure, including my mother, who used to talk about her as if she was one of the family. Eventually we found out who she was. The house had belonged to a Madame Mueller, an actress who had died there alone with her dog. There were some old photographs of her – and I recognized the person I had seen; it was her all right.

'After I eventually sold the house and moved into a modern flat in Salford, I had two guests in one day and one said to me, "Have you got an old lady staying with you? I've just seen her go past the door carrying a bowl of soup!" So perhaps my old friend followed me,' said Pat Phoenix. 'And I don't mind a bit!'

In 1972 a hundred-year-old antique shop in Northenden Road was the scene of apparent poltergeist activity witnessed by an assistant, Les Norton, who is reported to have been so shattered by the experience that he resigned his job and vowed never to return. In his room at the top of the shop Les had suddenly begun to feel cold and, thinking that the door must have been left open, he turned round – and saw a small wooden chair which stood against the wall begin to wobble towards him, inching forwards a little at a time, as if propelled by an invisible hand.

Terrified, Les raced for the door but before he could get out of the room a vase of flowers lifted itself from a table and crashed to pieces on the floor. Les telephoned his parents at Altrincham and the police station at Sale. Shortly afterwards a police sergeant and a constable arrived on the scene and as they entered the room they noticed a strange, clammy coldness, although the fire was burning to capacity. While he had been out of the room some photographs had fallen to the floor from their place on top of the television set. The policemen noticed that a dog and a cat belonging to the shop seemed to be showing signs of undue fright.

Les Norton said nothing of the sort had ever happened to him previously although on many occasions he had heard nocturnal footsteps when he had slept in the room; at the time he had decided that the neighbours must be responsible — now he was not so sure.

Salford, GREATER MANCHESTER

When the Victoria Theatre closed its doors for the last time in February 1972 there was considerable local speculation as to what would happen to the theatre's ghost, a Lady in White.

The ghost is thought to be that of a programme seller at the theatre in the early days of this century. She fell in love with a leading actor but he rejected her and she threw herself from the balcony to her death. Her name was Phyllis and, whatever the origin, a ghostly female figure in white was seen at the theatre many times, usually by women members of the staff. Aubrey Phillips, who produced the last season of shows at the theatre, said at the time: 'I remember in the days when we did repertory an elderly actress who knew nothing about the story was so frightened of the place that she ran out into the street. She was psychic, she said, and sensed there was something there. More recently a barmaid we had ran downstairs one night, scared out of her wits. She said the figure of a woman had come into the bar through one wall and disappeared through another. We reassured her and she went back to work. But the Lady in

White appeared in the bar again that night and this time the poor barmaid was too upset to go back. In fact she gave up the job.'

Next door to the theatre, separated only by a connecting wall, the Irwell Castle Hotel also has a ghost, a strange shadowy figure. The licensee, Mrs Sally Dunnet, talked about the peculiar happenings at the time the Victoria Theatre was closing. 'We've been here four and a half years but I didn't see anything until about a year ago. It looked like the head and shoulders of a person about five feet six inches tall, but I have never been able to distinguish any features. It's like seeing someone through a pane of frosted glass. But I have seen it frequently, as often as three times a week just recently. It always comes in through the back and in fact I've often sent someone out to see if there is anyone there.'

The publication of these experiences in the *Manchester Evening News* revived memories for some of the newspaper's readers, including Mr D. Cameron of Heaton Chapel, who was stage manager at the theatre for a period in the early 1960s. 'I had many visits from this lady while I was working in the theatre, on so many occasions in fact that we took her for granted. You could tell when she had been around as there was always a smell of perfume. On three occasions I saw her and at other times I heard her moving about. This may sound silly but I became quite attached to her and when I was working on the sets at night I would look forward to seeing her around. Most of my stage crew knew about her and we've all had a laugh when someone from outside saw her ... may she rest in peace.'

In March 1972, Mrs Dorothy Gresty of Higher Irlam related a legend that her grandmother had told her about the Victoria Theatre, a story suggesting that the two hauntings may be related. In the early years of the theatre there was trouble between a member of the theatre staff, his girlfriend and a young actor. The girl set her cap at the actor and a row flared up when the boyfriend found them together upstairs in the empty theatre after hours. No one knows what really happened in the balcony but it seems that the girl toppled over to her death. It is more than likely that in those days the public house next door would be a convenient place to meet and eat and it must be within the bounds of possibility that the male figure seen at the Irwell Castle Hotel could be the man who caused the death of poor Phyllis, perhaps popping next door almost immediately afterwards.

In 1959 considerable local interest centred on disturbances at a house in Tully Street: unexplained happenings that resulted in examination of the property by officials from the Gas Board, the Water Board, the Town Hall and Salford Police Station. Yet no rational explanation was discovered.

The strange affair began on Christmas Eve, 1959, and continued unabated for almost two months, when a half-hour service of exorcism seemed to mark the end of the disturbances, although in the manner of poltergeists, it may well have been that the entity had expended its energy and run its course.

So violent and loud were the noises at the height of the trouble that they were heard in every house in the street. Sometimes the sounds resembled heavy hammering; at other times they put those who heard them in mind of a heavy cannonball bouncing on the ceiling. At one stage a psychic researcher from Manchester believed that the sounds represented a code and that they might be an effort to convey some kind of message or communicate in some way with one of the members of the family, most likely the twelve-year-old son of the occupants. Although the boy seemed quite indifferent to the noises, he may still have been used in some unknown way.

The extraordinary affair received considerable publicity and crowds of people constantly thronged the street and collected outside the affected house in the hope of seeing the ghost, although no visible entity was ever reported during the Tully Street manifestations.

One visitor was the Reverend Edward Dimond, the vicar of St James's Church, Broughton, and having repeatedly heard the noises himself, he was convinced that they had a supernatural origin and were the result of 'a restless and resentful spirit'. Accordingly, he made application to the Bishop of Manchester for permission to hold a service of exorcism at the house to 'persuade the trouble-causer to desist and leave the occupants in peace'. Following the service, all was quiet at Tully Street and another 'poltergeist' had arrived, manifested itself for a set period, and then departed as mysteriously and as suddenly as it had appeared.

Kersal Cell, an interesting partly timbered house that was the birthplace of John Byrom (1692-1763), the poet who wrote 'Christians Awake', was previously a religious house attached to Zenton Priory and it is probably from this period that the ghost of the eight-hundred-year-old house belongs, for it is the form of a greyish monk that wanders about these old rooms and most frequently, it is said, at Christmastide and at the turn of the year.

Saltney, CHESHIRE

In the days when Mr K. R. Jones of Blacon was a lad of fifteen, there used to be a spectral cyclist near Saltney Junction railway station.

One of his duties in those days was for the lad to wake up local railway guards and very early one morning, after waking up a guard who lived in Sandy Lane, he was on his way back to the office when he saw the light of a cycle coming towards him. He heard the squeaking cycle chain and he saw a figure riding it, but when it was within twenty feet of him it suddenly vanished. Next morning he made the same journey at the same time and again the same thing happened.

On the third morning he chanced to be accompanied by a guard at this point and they both saw and heard exactly the same yet again. First the light of the bicycle, then the sound of the squeaking chain, then the figure visible on the bicycle and, when less than twenty feet distant, the whole thing vanishing.

Some time later Mr Jones discovered that a man who used to work on the railway and who rode a bicycle had hanged himself at the railway junction.

Sefton, MERSEYSIDE

The Punch Bowl Inn is said to be haunted and many strange stories of strange happenings there have been published over the years. In 1973 the reputed ghost of a sailor who died four hundred years earlier was seen by Mrs Peggy Wilding of Crosby.

Mrs Wilding never believed in ghosts – until New Year's Eve, 1973, when she saw one. She was on an upstairs landing of the inn at the time and when she saw the mist-enshrouded head and shoulders of a young man, seemingly floating in the air in front of her, she ran down the stairs to call a member of the staff. When they went back upstairs the figure had vanished. When she first saw the form, Peggy Wilding thought it was her own reflection in a window and then she realized that it could not be so, for the face was of course that of a young man. She was very frightened by the experience but no longer scoffs at people who say they have seen ghosts.

A waitress at the Punch Bowl Inn saw the form of a man, dressed in sailors' clothes, sitting in the corner of the rear room on the ground floor, a room known as the News Room. The figure was sitting in the corner by the fireplace in the comfortably furnished and pleasant room which has none of the atmosphere one might expect in a haunted room. Other members of the staff have seen the same figure in the same place. Staff and customers have seen doors open by themselves and have heard footsteps late at night when no one is responsible. One witness says she was pushed down the stairs by a phantom form.

Some of the regular customers have some very odd stories to relate. One man insists that he was dragged off his bicycle in the car park by an invisible figure; another says he was sitting in the bar one afternoon when someone came running in wanting to know who was digging a grave in the nearby churchyard. The man said that he had seen a figure, dressed in blue breeches like an old-fashioned seaman, apparently digging away at an unmarked grave. The man led the regular customer out of the inn and to the churchyard. There was no one about but by the grave where the figure had been seen there was a pile of fresh earth.

According to local tradition, centuries ago the Irish Sea reached almost to the Punch Bowl Inn, at that time a rectory, and records show that the bodies of sailors have been washed ashore near the inn. The rear room – or News Room – was then used as a mortuary and the bodies of these sailors were later buried in Sefton churchyard. Could the ghost be one of these unfortunate sailors? The daughter of the manager in 1973 was among those who claimed to have seen the ghost.

Southport, MERSEYSIDE

A curious historical case concerns the Reverend Robert Bee and his wife, who spent a holiday at Southport in December 1873, staying with Mrs Bee's parents. On the first day after their arrival, a day spent pleasantly enough walking about the town, the couple had their evening meal and then settled down to a game of chess. It was a pastime they both enjoyed but this evening for some reason neither the rector nor his wife seemed to be able to concentrate on the game and at length they put the board and chessmen away. It was now about seven-thirty and Mrs Bee went downstairs to speak to her mother. About twenty minutes later Mr Bee, noticing that the time was ten minutes to eight, walked out of the drawing-room where he and his wife had been sitting and emerged on to the landing.

There, much to his surprise, he came face to face with a lady who appeared from nowhere; she was dressed as though she was going out and she hastily brushed past the astonished clergyman and hurried down the stairs ahead of him. Mr Bee was completely mystified for he had been told that the only people in the house were himself, his wife and his wife's parents. He was about to follow the figure downstairs when he saw his wife ascending the staircase and he immediately asked who the lady could be. Mrs Bee expressed surprise at the question and asserted that no one had passed her on the stairs and there was certainly no one in the house other than themselves and her parents.

Mr Bee was very puzzled for not only had he encountered the mysterious lady on the landing where she had brushed past him but he had also seen the figure pass his wife on the stairs! Both Mr and Mrs Bee went downstairs and talked with Mrs Bee's mother and again they were told that they were the only people in the house and no one could have entered the house without being seen.

The little episode would probably have been completely forgotten had not a telegram arrived for Mr Bee from Lincolnshire the following morning, informing him that his mother had died the previous evening. As a result Mr and Mrs Bee left Southport on the first available train. After the funeral Mr Bee asked his brother the exact time of their mother's death and learned that it was ten minutes to eight, the precise time that he had seen the strange figure. Mr Bee also learned that his mother had been taken ill in the street, wearing her accustomed outdoor wear and he suddenly realized that the clothing of the figure he had passed on the landing was exactly the same as that worn by his mother.

A very different type of psychic manifestation took place in 1969 when a team of demolition men were working on the thousand-room Palace Hotel, Birkside. Joseph Smith and eleven of his workmen all heard eerie voices and saw the four-ton lift move up and down by itself. The sounds of whispering were repeatedly heard in one particular corridor and in a suite of upper rooms and while this was disturbing enough, coupled with the strangely unpleasant atmosphere, most disturbing of all was the inexplicable behaviour of the lift. Once, as they entered the hotel, nine of the workmen together saw the doors of the lift slam shut and the car ascend to the second floor. The hotel was completely deserted at the time and furthermore electrical supplies had been totally cut off weeks earlier.

Investigators from the North Wales Electricity Board stated, after making full on-the-spot examination and enquiries: 'There isn't an amp of power going into the place.' The workmen, knowing full well that no known power was working the lift, ran up to the winding room and discovered the brake to be still in the 'on' position which should have prevented the lift from moving either up or down. They cut the inch-thick cables which supported the lift, but still it stayed where it was; they cut through the cables supporting the counter balance but still the lift did not budge; finally they used heavy hammers and crowbars to prise away the lift's guide bars and then, to the cheers of the relieved workmen, the lift crashed down to the pit at the bottom of the shaft and buried itself several feet into the ground.

The history of the hundred-and-twelve-year-old hotel holds no obvious explanations for a haunting although one story suggests that the architect had committed suicide by jumping from the top landing (where odd noises and an eerie atmosphere was reported) to fall to his death on the spot where the lift later stood. At one period of its history the hotel was used as a reception centre for the victims of a tragedy at sea and some of those rescued had died in the hotel, but not on the top floor. Another interesting aspect of this case lies in the fact that it was noticed that no dog or cat could be persuaded to visit the top landing. Time and again one of the demolition team had no difficulty in getting his dog to follow him all over the building, during the hours of daylight or darkness, but whenever they approached the top landing, the dog would sit and alertly await his master's return.

The Crossens area of Southport, to the north, has several ghosts and ghostly phenomena including spectral hoofbeats, a woman with a basket, a dark and rustling figure and strange knocking and banging noises. One of the occupants of Causeway Farm used to say that her family often heard strange banging noises from three rooms in the house but no door was ever found ajar, nor window open that might have caused the noise. At Rectory Farm there used to be a horse-box that some people thought was haunted and many people, not knowing its reputation, would comment on the uneasy and disturbing feeling that they noticed when they were near the box. Older local people talked in whispers of the strange and shadowy shape of a woman, wearing a white cap and carrying a basket that has been seen crossing the farmyard and the road from the direction of where the horse-box stood, a figure that was seen one night by Mrs B. Rimmer's brother when he went out into the yard to fetch some coal: he ran back empty-handed for he had met the silent figure in the yard. Neighbours too said they saw the figure of a woman with a basket flitting across the road. One said that a friend of hers watched the figure from a distance of a few yards, thinking for a moment that it was someone he knew; she looked back at him over her shoulder and suddenly he felt very frightened although he could never explain exactly why for he couldn't plainly see her face.

The softly rustling ghost used to be heard near the old ferry at Ralph's Wife's Lane and if you waited, it was said, you might see the dark form of a woman dressed in the fashion of George IV, a black-clad figure, thought to be the ghost of a woman drowned in the floods of 1834. This ghost was never seen to approach any house or building; she was always observed near the river, usually walking towards it but sometimes coming up from the river and walking in the direction of Banks.

No one, it seems, has ever claimed to see the spectral steeds whose hoofbeats are said to echo across the countryside as they race through the darkness. Then, just before dawn, they are heard returning, but where they come from and where they go to nobody knows.

Meols Hall has two ghosts: the apparition of a priest in brown robes that is said to parade periodically, and the murderer of 'Old Nancy' or 'Old Chip Bonnet', as 'genuine and authentic a spectre as any manorial ghost can possibly be', according to a report published in 1934.

A chip bonnet was a bonnet made out of straw and the ghost of Old Nancy is linked with a story of buried treasure that is supposed to have been washed up on Churchdown shore from a wrecked Spanish ship that foundered there. Old Nancy, an eccentric local inhabitant, found the treasure and hid it but some ill-disposed tenant of Meols Hall, endeavouring to gain possession of the valuables, managed to inveigle the old woman into the Hall and there he pushed her down the stairs, causing her fatal injuries. Yet she died without disclosing where she had hidden the treasure and the ghost of her murderer still walks up and down the stairs, seeking the treasure that he is doomed never to find.

In February 1977 the present owner of Meols Hall, Colonel Roger Fleetwood Hesketh, told me the only legendary ghost story – slightly different to that above – connected with this house that he had heard of. As he put it, 'In the eighteenth and early part of the nineteenth century the Heskeths of North Meols lived at Rossall Hall (inherited from the Fleetwood family), while Meols Hall was occupied for several generations by members of the Linakin family, their resident agents. At some time during their period of occupation a ship was wrecked on the coast, and a box containing the possessions of an old lady who was among the survivors was brought to this house. When she came to collect it, the person she spoke to disclaimed all knowledge of its existence, whereupon she placed a curse on the house and its occupants, and according to the story has haunted the drive ever since. She is known locally as "Chip Bonnet". I have never seen her myself, nor have I ever met anyone who has, so perhaps the curse has now been lifted!'

Speke, MERSEYSIDE

The original Speke Hall, now an interesting black and white National Trust property south-west of Liverpool, was built late in the fifteenth century and over the years it has been added to and altered to suit the needs and preferences of succeeding generations. The ghost, a White Lady, is thought to be the unhappy Mary Norris (the Norris family had built Speke Hall) who married 'Worthless' Lord Beauclerk, an inveterate gambler, possibly descended from Charles II and Nell Gwynn. The Lady Beauclerk had not long given birth when her husband announced that his recklessness had resulted in ruin and in her overwrought state the anguished lady threw her infant from the window of the Tapestry Room to its death in the moat below before rushing down to the Great Hall and committing suicide.

The Curator of Speke Hall, Mr P. W. G. Lawson, tells me that the Tapestry or Haunted Bedroom is in the northern range of the house, built in 1598, and has been reputed to be haunted since at least the middle years of the nineteenth century. The Watt family, who owned the house from about 1795 to 1921, seem to have been sufficiently impressed with the story of the distraught Lady Beauclerk to have acquired, in the nineteenth century, a large cradle which still stands in the Tapestry Room.

Known historical facts however do not support the story. Not only do the Beauclerks seem to have only visited Speke occasionally but Lady Mary Beauclerk died in 1766 in the parish of St George, Great Hanover Square – some twenty-two years after Lord Sidney (1703-44). Their only child,

Topham Beauclerk (1739-80), survived to inherit the property.

However, the Curator added, the fact that recorded history does not support the popular story associated with Speke does not necessarily mean that there is not some presence in the Tapestry Room, as various people interested in such phenomena have maintained that they have experienced disconcerting sensations in the room, including Miss Adelaide Watt who, as reported by my old friend Alasdair Alpin MacGregor, observed a ghost in the room that disappeared into the wall, close to a window.

Stalybridge, GREATER MANCHESTER

In March 1977, in the company of Mrs Vera Bottomley, Freda and Steuart Kiernander and my wife Joyce, I visited the secondary modern school for boys that was originally the home of a mill owner named Harrison, a house that he called West Hill, the name of the present school.

Mrs Vera Bottomley, who lives in Stalybridge, told us that she can remember as a child knowing the only surviving member of this family, an old, shuffling woman of about eighty, usually dressed in a long fur coat and conspicuous by her untidy appearance. She never married and at that time lived in a much smaller house in another part of the town.

One night a few years ago, the caretaker of the school, who lived on the premises, was awakened by the strange behaviour of his dog. He went downstairs and found the animal whining and cowering in the hall. As he was speaking to the dog he saw a woman walking towards a blank wall. He called to her to tell her that she couldn't get out that way, thinking at the time how very strange that she should be in the building at that time of night. She just walked straight through the wall and disappeared!

The caretaker had only worked at the school for a short while and he wasn't a local man. He always maintained that he didn't even know about the Harrison family having once owned the house but his vivid description of the woman and the way she was dressed left no doubt in the minds of one or two elderly people who had known her in her younger days that he had indeed seen the ghost of Miss Harrison. The dog, a ferocious animal treated with great respect by the schoolboys, behaved in a similar manner several times afterwards.

It was in March 1976 that Mrs Vera Bottomley wrote to me about a strange event that had befallen her and her cousin Jessie forty years before, in the Brushes Valley, and in March 1977 she showed us exactly where this unique and never-to-be-forgotten encounter took place.

Vera was then nineteen and her cousin a couple of years younger. At that time her uncle, Jessie's father, lived in a cottage at the foot of the Pennine Range, actually within the boundary of Stalybridge. Vera had stayed the night at the cottage on this occasion and the following morning, a Sunday in the middle of summer, the two girls set off for a walk over the moors.

This part of the moor is called the Brushes Valley and there are four reservoirs, one rising above the other to the open moorland. Beside the reservoirs runs a road and it was on this road, near the third reservoir, that the strange event took place.

The girls were sauntering leisurely along, enjoying the summer weather and talking of commonplace things – but let Vera tell her own story: 'I can assure you we were not thinking of anything remotely supernatural when suddenly we heard music and although we could see a stretch of road for about a quarter of a mile, almost immediately there descended upon us two young men in full Highland attire – sporran, kilt, Glengarry – and both playing bagpipes and playing them very expertly too. We stepped to the side of the narrow road and they swung by us and disappeared round a bend in the road in the direction we had just come.

'We were dumbfounded and to appreciate the atmosphere you would have had to be there! We talked about this experience many times over the years and we both agreed that two things struck us as very odd. First, the abrupt and sudden way in which the two figures appeared and secondly, the fact that neither as much as glanced at either of us. The occurrence took place before the war and when we made enquiries about soldiers being in the vicinity it was said to be extremely unlikely, and anyway, no one else had heard or seen anything unusual even though there were isolated cottages in the area.'

Mrs Bottomley was good enough to obtain special permission for us all to visit the scene of this odd and obviously genuine experience; she also told us that she had recently discovered that there was evidence that 'Bonnie' Prince Charlie spent at least one night in the vicinity, staying at the old Manor House that dates back to the seventeenth century, before travelling north. Having met Mrs Vera Bottomley and visited the scene of this strange encounter in her company, I believe she and her cousin may well have been fortunate enough to have experienced genuine spontaneous paranormal activity: to have glimpsed for a moment, as if through a slit in the curtain of time, something that happened more than two-hundred-and-fifty years before.

Stockport, GREATER MANCHESTER

The old Britannia Inn on Churchgate was reported to have a ghost in February 1966, soon after the inn was taken over by Mr Bill Smith, a businessman who set about using the Britannia and an adjoining building for his carpet manufacturing. A covered bridge connected the two properties, the door of which was covered by plaster. The cellar of the adjoining building was locked and obviously unused but when the door was broken down and the floor found to be uneven and duly levelled, next day everything in the building had been disturbed; even some timber was moved.

Later one of the workers refused to enter the building alone after she had found a cat frightened out of its wits by something invisible to her. This woman's reaction was followed by the rest of the staff and the idea of the building being used for manufacturing purposes had to be abandoned. It has been suggested that a very deep well under the cellar may be responsible for some of the 'strange' noises, caused by water and air pressure every time there was a lot of rain; this might well have accounted also for movement of the cellar floor but it seems a little difficult to explain a gas pipe ripped from a wall in terms of air pressure.

In 1956 Miss Enid Millward told me that following the discovery of hidden rooms at her fascinating Staircase Café, she and her guests were disturbed by phantom footsteps and the sounds of movement.

'It is as though someone is trying to get out,' she said. She instanced 'a rapping and a sound like footsteps that seems to come from the ceiling . . .'

During June 1956 workmen who were decorating the new dining-room discovered an extension of the staircase and found that it led to three previously hidden rooms, and it is from these rooms that Miss Millward was convinced that the noises originated.

The Staircase Café is justly famous for its hand-carved staircase, walled-up for years and only discovered in 1955. Mr W. S. Gilbert, at that time curator of the Vernon Park Museum, estimated that the building was at least three hundred years old; the walls, underneath the plaster, were made of wattle and daub, and a Jacobean fireplace in one of the rooms bears the date 1618.

Local historians believe that Lord Elcho stayed in these premises in 1745 when, as Commander of 'Bonnie' Prince Charlie's Life Guards, he led the flight of the Prince's army after its disastrous defeat at Derby. According to historical records he reached Stockport on a Saturday night in December, seized a number of townspeople as hostages, including the Constable of Stockport (who was suspected of giving information to the enemy) and carried them off to Manchester with him. But he spent a night in Stockport with a detachment of troops on guard, staying at 'an excellent house in the Market Place'. Miss Millward was never worried by the noises. 'They certainly didn't frighten me; it is just that I am very curious as to their origin and if it is a ghost I am sure we can get along fine...'

A ghost may have been photographed at the Thatched House, a public house in Spring Gardens. In 1966 the licensees, Mary and Bob Jackson, showed me a photograph of a former employee, Thomas Heywood, now dead, and on the blank wall behind the subject another face can be distinguished. Relatives of the dead man say that it is Thomas Heywood's grandfather and point to the distinctive high forehead, the bulbous nose, the beard and the high wing-collar. Sceptics and photographic experts suggest that the 'face' is a freak of some kind, possibly a curious representation of a painting on the wall behind; Bob and Mary Jackson say there was nothing on the wall behind and this has since been wallpapered but if there is some such natural explanation why should the mystery face be so readily recognized by Thomas Heywood's relatives as his grandfather?

In the middle of 1975 the occupants of No. 15 Wirral Crescent, Gorsey Bank, said the house was haunted. They had repeatedly heard the crying of a baby, although there was no baby in the house, nor had there ever been one; the figure of a tall and ugly man with a disturbing presence had been seen; no pets would stay in the house and freezing cold draughts blew through centrally-heated rooms.

Cath and Colin Pritchard and their two boys, Desmond and Sean, all experienced the strange happenings and so did Mrs Pritchard's mother, Mrs Lily Higgins. She baby-sat for the couple one evening and said afterwards 'If this house was blessed a thousand times, I wouldn't stay again.' The Pritchards were later returning home on that occasion than they had expected and Mrs Higgins decided to stay the night. She retired to the spare bedroom where she had spent scores of undisturbed nights but this one was to be different. She had only been asleep a short time when she found herself awake and aware of a presence. She looked round the room and saw the figure of a man with his arms outstretched, walking slowly towards her. 'It was so incredibly clear,' she told Stuart Rigby of the *Stockport Express*, 'and his face was uglier than anything I have ever seen in my life. Lumps of flesh were hanging off him. He stood over me, his hands reaching for my neck and I found that I was paralysed and speechless with fear. I couldn't even scream. It seemed to last for about five minutes and then the figure disappeared.'

One day Cath called her seven-year-old son Desmond to tell him it was tea time. He was playing in his room on the first floor. As she called up the stairs she heard the sound of a baby crying. Afterwards she learned that at least three neighbours had heard the sound of a crying baby emanating from the house – at a time when the Pritchard family had all been out. Each time one of the neighbours went to the house to see whether she could help and each time the crying noise stopped as soon as anyone approached the front door. In his room, on this occasion, Desmond was playing with his toys when the door opened and a tall man walked in. Desmond felt very frightened; he had never seen the man before but he knew that he had to get away. He instinctively shrank back to the window – still the figure came on and Desmond, knowing that at all costs he had to get away from that 'nasty man', jumped out of the window, breaking both legs. The same form was seen shortly afterwards but no one seems to know who the ghost is or why such a horrible and disturbing spectre haunted the house.

A black taxi-cab stood for months at the rear of Ray Normansell's office home in Lowfield Road, unused because it was thought to be haunted. None of the ten drivers occupied in the private hire business would drive it or even sit in it.

The reputation that the cab acquired can be pin-pointed to 30 November 1974, when the cab was being driven by Brian Mohan along the A6 road through Great Moor after taking a fare to Whaley Bridge. He had just passed Woodsmoor pedestrian crossing when Brian thought he saw a movement in his mirror reflecting the rear seat of the cab; he glanced at the interior mirror and then blinked in surprise for he saw in his mirror the reflection of an old woman sitting on the back seat. At the time he thought there must be some obvious explanation, a curious reflection or something of the kind, and he looked back to the road ahead and continued on past Stockport Convent.

As he approached the Davenport Theatre he took a long look into the mirror. The figure of the old woman was still there. She was sitting upright, quite motionless and without anything striking about her – even her expression conveyed nothing to Brian, an experienced driver who began to be very puzzled by the silent figure for he knew he had not picked up a fare since leaving Whaley Bridge.

Brian thought back over the evening. He had had nothing to drink; he was not in need of sleep; he was not hungry and he had had nothing to cause him to see things that were not there. Yet there was the woman sitting impassively in the back of his cab. He decided to see exactly what she was up to.

He drove past the next crossing, at Stockport Grammar School, and then suddenly pulled into the side of the road and stopped. He pulled down the glass partition and turned to face his mysterious passenger. The cab was empty! He got out of his driving seat, walked all round the cab and looked up and down the street. There was no sign of the old woman he had seen seconds before in the back of his cab.

In December 1974 Brian Mohan told his story to Stuart Rigby of the *Stockport Express*. 'I saw her both when we were in darkness, at the Convent, and when it was light,' he said. 'So it can't have been an image. No one could have jumped into the cab because of the noise of the door and the interior light. We've spent hours trying to work out what it could be but we haven't come up with any answers. I know it wasn't just me seeing things because I looked three times to make sure and she was there each time.'

Ray Normansell speaks highly of all his drivers and Brian Mohan is no exception. 'He's not the kind of man who would concoct such a story. When he came back that night, he was as white as a sheet – he really saw something that frightened him.'

Brian Mohan described the mysterious figure he saw in his cab as a woman aged between fifty and sixty with long and thick hair. She wore a black overcoat with a pointed collar, a frilly white blouse and a black bow. He is quite sure that he would recognize the woman if he ever saw her again but he hopes he does not do so, for she cost him several restless nights and he has no intention of using that particular cab again.

The Wright's Arms at Offerton was said to be haunted in 1970 by the landlord, Mr Robert Higginbotham, and his wife Mary; they had taken over the public house in 1968 and ever since they had been at the Wright's Arms they had heard mysterious tapping noises, footsteps echoing through the premises when the place was deserted late at night, floorboards creaking when there was no one near them and doors opening and closing by themselves.

'I do think there is something here,' Robert Higginbotham told me at the time. 'But I'd like to see it with my own eyes before I believe it.' Although he had seen nothing to worry him, apart from a swinging door, Robert certainly heard more than enough to convince him that the noises had an intensity and almost an intelligence that ruled out such explanations as woodwork cooling and pipes expanding or contracting.

When they first moved into the premises Robert slept

downstairs on a camp bed and time after time he was awakened by the sound of footsteps and would have sworn that someone was in the place, but as soon as he moved the noises ceased and he never found any explanation.

The Higginbothams's alsatian dog, Meg, showed a healthy respect for the ghost – or whatever it was. She used to be quite vicious in the early days but she quietened down a lot later on, although sometimes she would whine when the knocking started and she always preferred the ground floor to upstairs.

The building is something like four hundred and fifty years old, so it has had plenty of time to acquire a ghost and far from being scared the Higginbothams, on the whole, were not bothered by the affair which they were never able to explain satisfactorily.

The banks of the River Goyt at Otterspool are said to be haunted by the ghost of John Bradshaw's daughter. Bradshaw presided over the council that condemned Charles I to death (and his ghost haunts the Inslip Rooms in the deanery at Westminster Abbey where the trial was held) but his daughter is supposed to have fallen in love with a Royalist officer who, while acting as a messenger for the King, had the audacity to call at Marple Hall, owned by John's brother Henry, to see his beloved. One of the Bradshaws discovered what was happening and, waiting until the officer was fording the river at Otterspool, had the man set upon and killed. So the girl Bradshaw walks the quiet banks bewailing the loss of her lover.

For more than twenty years St George's Vicarage was 'haunted' by the sound of footsteps – and perhaps it still is. Canon Wilfrid Garlick tells me that he and his wife lived at the Vicarage for twenty-six years and the phenomenon – whatever it was – started fairly soon after they moved into the twenty-two roomed house in 1948. The footsteps seemed to originate from an empty attic. In the beginning Mrs Garlick might be in the sitting-room and her husband in the study when the noises were heard. Each assumed the noises were made by the other, but on enquiry it was found that neither of them had entered the attic. They would search and search and search but they never discovered anything or saw anything.

Gradually they became accustomed to hearing footsteps for which they could find no rational explanation although, as Canon Garlick pointed out to me, 'neither of us is given to this sort of thing' and having failed to find any cause for the footsteps, heard by both of them time after time, they began to refer to 'it' as 'the Archdeacon' after their predecessor but one, a formidable man, Archdeacon Thorpe, the first incumbent of St George's, who lived there from 1897 to 1936. One of his descendants is the Liberal MP, Jeremy Thorpe.

Such comments as 'It's the Archdeacon at it again' became commonplace. The sound was quite definitely that of footsteps and always they seemed to come from the same place but they were heard at all sorts of times. An explanation in terms of water pipes, creaking floorboards and doors or windows rattling was sought but it 'just wasn't that sort of noise'.

There was no question of any ghost being seen or feeling cold spots or temperature changes and there was no element of fear; in fact the Garlicks thought the whole thing rather comical and it gave them plenty of laughs.

The other interesting thing is that sometimes the strange and quite inexplicable sound would disappear for months on end and nothing remotely resembling footsteps would be heard; then 'off it would go again'.

It was noticed that the disturbances were heard most frequently at times of crisis for the Thorpe family and Canon Garlick tells me they had 'a real visitation when Jeremy Thorpe's wife was killed and again when Sir Geoffry [sic] Christie Miller [Archdeacon Thorpe's son-in-law] died at sea, and that time it went on until we held his memorial service ... he was buried at sea ... again when the husband of one of Thorpe's daughters died, and again when she died...'

Canon and Mrs Garlick have always emphasized that they never found the noises in the least disturbing, just curious. 'Perhaps after attributing it, rightly or wrongly, to the old chap we felt it could hardly be other than benevolent.' Only once or twice did other people think they heard anything and, as the Canon points out, it could easily have been because they were aware of the story. Canon Wilfrid Garlick told me in January 1977 that his successor at the Vicarage had then been there about eighteen months and says he hasn't heard the footsteps so far. The attic, where the footsteps seem to originate, was the maid's room when Archdeacon Thorpe was alive.

St Thomas's Hospital, in common with many hospitals up and down the country, is reputed to have a ghostly 'White Lady' and in January 1977 I was in touch with Mrs M. K. Glynn, the Nursing Officer, who told me she had worked in the hospital for thirty-four years and had never seen the 'White Lady', but certainly there had been many rumours. She mentioned some sort of investigation into the mysteries, conducted by a previous superintendent at the hospital. I then contacted Mr Wilfred Tattum but he told me he retired in 1962 after being at St Thomas's for twenty-three years and he 'never, at any time, heard any references to the 'White Lady' during the whole time he was at the hospital. He did tell me that the premises were built as a workhouse in 1841. At one time Mr Tattum did carry out 'a great deal of research' about developments during the preceding hundred years, but he never heard any references to ghosts.

On the other hand a leading article in the local *Stockport Express*, dated 31 October 1974, goes into considerable detail about the ghost and states, 'Former hospital superintendent Mr Wilfred Tattum came under so much pressure to discover the nature of the phenomena that he instituted an enquiry'. According to this article the ghostly White Lady, 'as she was known to scores of night nurses and sisters who saw her and can still testify to it, always appeared at night in precisely the same place'.

The phantom figure is described as being of average height, wearing robe-like apparel and smiling in a kindly manner. Usually the form seemed to hover some way above ground level and was often surrounded by 'an intense light'. The appearance of the figure was haphazard and she might appear at any time of the day or night and remain visible for a variable length of time. Her identity was never reliably defined.

A former night sister at St Thomas's 'now retired and highly respected' told the following to the author of the newspaper article, under a guarantee of anonymity: 'I had served at the hospital for about two months and had been told all about the White Lady, but of course I thought it was a figment of imagination. However, I was doing a round at 2 a.m. one morning and I suddenly stopped in my tracks as I saw it. It was exactly as had been described. Now I am not the type of person with clouds in my head. I am absolutely down to earth but I saw that figure. And I saw it quite a few times after that occasion.'

The *Stockport Express* article goes on to say that the 'apparition' always appeared in a place where there was air all round it, 'it never moved, changed position, spoke or became transparent and at times it was witnessed by more than one nurse at one time'.

A final paragraph on the White Lady of St Thomas's says that 'scores of nurses . . . deduced and firmly believed that a visit from the White Lady was a forecast of death'. As far as I can establish the whole 'haunting' of St Thomas's Hospital rests with the author of the *Stockport Express* article; try as I may I have been unable to find anyone who says the place is haunted.

Tarporley, CHESHIRE

There is a lane between Tarporley and Tiverton that is haunted by a ghostly man and a ghostly dog.

One calm September evening in 1971 Mr A. Pressick of Handbridge drove two girls from a Chester discotheque to their home in Tiverton. Taking what he thought was a short cut on the way home he became lost, but then ahead of him in the country lane he saw a man walking his dog and he decided to ask the way.

As he drew closer he saw that the man seemed to be dressed in a khaki smock tied at the waist, loose khaki trousers tied below the knee with string and a sou'wester-type hat. The dog was on a string lead. He also noticed, somewhat to his surprise, that both man and dog seemed to be walking into a very strong head wind: the saliva of the dog as it pulled on the lead was blowing backwards and the man's body appeared to be straining against the wind; yet it was a very calm night.

As he drew abreast of the pair Mr Pressick stopped the car and leaned over the passenger seat, lowered the window and asked whether he was travelling in the right direction for Tarporley. The man made no reply and walked on down the road. Mr Pressick drew level with him again and repeated his enquiry, shouting this time as he thought the man might be deaf. He was a matter of only five or six inches from the figure and this time the man turned and looked at him. His glaring eyes and curious complexion were rather frightening in the circumstances and still he made no reply. Turning away he walked on and Mr Pressick watched him, suddenly conscious of the sound of wind.

He began to think there was something distinctly odd about the figure and he drove off quickly, looking back in his driving mirror after he had passed the figure but he could see no sign of either man or dog. He did notice a very tall hedge on that side of the road but there was no break in it and he was at a loss to account for the sudden disappearance of both figures.

Later he made enquiries and learned that years ago an old farmer had been knocked down and killed in the lane by a coach. His dog had also been killed and there was a storm raging at the time.

Thurstaston, MERSEYSIDE

Thurstaston Hall, as the present owner, Colonel R. G. Turner, tells me, dates back in parts to about 1350, although most of it consists of additions made in 1680 with a further wing added in 1836. In the 1350 portion there is a room leading off the main staircase, still with its original beams, that is supposed to be haunted.

For nearly nine hundred years the manor has never been sold, passing from the Norman noble either by inheritance or bequest through the Haselwells, the Whitmores, the Gleggs and the present family of Turner. The hall, a fascinating maze of a place, delightful and hallowed and full of history, has an unusual acquisition: a sketch of a ghost.

It seems that a well-known portrait painter, Reginald Easton, staying at the Hall in the latter half of the last century was engaged in painting a portrait of a member of the family then in residence. The artist slept in the room since regarded as haunted and one night, or rather very early one morning, he heard the bedroom door open and saw, standing in the doorway, an old woman wringing her hands in evident distress. She approached the astonished artist and stood at the foot of the four-poster without speaking or making any sound. He asked her what she wanted and, since she seemed to be in great trouble, offered help, but she only passed round the bed, made her way to the bell-pull (which she appeared to pull) and then she vanished.

Several times after that Reginald Easton saw the same

figure. It always acted in exactly the same way and it never spoke or gave any intimation of seeing him or being aware of his presence. He, for his part, was well aware of her presence and felt it to be supernatural in origin, yet he became used to the figure and lost all sense of fear of it. One night he took his sketch pad to bed with him and while the apparition was in the room he did a rough sketch which he afterwards completed.

Some time later a gentleman acquainted with the details of this story and with Easton's drawing was staying with some people in another part of England whose ancestors had once lived at Thurstaston Hall when he immediately recognized one of the family portraits as being identical to the sketch of the apparition made by the artist. He then learned that it was a family tradition that the subject of the portrait was supposed to haunt Thurstaston Hall.

When the facts were related to Reginald Easton he professed complete ignorance of the family concerned, the legend and the portrait which he had certainly never seen.

Colonel Turner tells me that as far as he knows nobody has seen the ghost since and certainly none of his family have seen or heard anything of a paranormal nature.

Up Holland, LANCASHIRE

More than seventy years ago some very strange occurrences took place in an old house in Church Street and I am indebted to a local historian, Jim Sharratt, for providing me with a great deal of fascinating information on this interesting case. Mr Sharratt tells me that he can just recall being taken by his father to see the 'Ghost House' when he was six years old.

It was in August 1904 that the village of Up Holland first became aware that a three-storied house next door to the ancient White Lion Inn and overlooking a churchyard, which had never been regarded as anything special, was in fact haunted. There were flashes of light, loud raps, mysterious noises and flying stones and plaster that could be seen and heard plainly outside the house. Before long crowds of people gathered night after night to witness the strange performances.

The 'haunted house' was occupied at the time by a widow, Mrs Winstanley, and her family of four sons and three daughters. Opposite lived a little girl of ten, then named Matthews and now Mrs J. Tennant, who almost lived with the Winstanleys, she spent so much time at the house. She related to Jim Sharratt her recollections of how the affair began:

'Mrs Winstanley wanted to fry some steak but could not get the fire going. Where the flames should have been *red*, they were of all colours. Mrs Winstanley thought that the girls – Maggie and herself – had put paraffin on to the fire. She was so angry with them that she chased them out of the house.

'Two of Mrs Winstanley's sons used to sleep in the 'Ghost Room' on the first floor, above the door; the right one of two windows looking at the house from the front, and although not on the ground floor of the house it was virtually on street level. There were bamboo rods with curtains to the window. The family went to bed in the evening of the day the fire wouldn't get going and during the night the bamboo rods and curtains fell on to the two brothers in bed. They put them back, but as often as they did so, so they fell again.

'Then one brick began to repeatedly fall out of the fireplace in the room where the two boys slept. It was preceded by three knocks. Then lights would flash in the room as if made by electricity or gas, but the house had neither. These flashing lights attracted the attention of neighbours, to whom they were clearly visible. On Sundays, it was noticed, three knocks would sound, then the brick would fall out, followed by a sound that resembled the syllable *cer* repeated twice at a time, *cer-cer*; in some ways the sound was like a person clearing his throat. This noise came to be regarded as a signal that the "ghost" was requesting silence. On this particular Sunday a large Bible lay on a bamboo table in the bedroom. When quiet had been restored by the *cer-cer* noise, the clasp of the Bible, a brass one, could be heard unfastening itself, followed by the sound of pages being turned. Suddenly the "ghost" would repeat several times: "Whither thou goest, I will go".'

Miss Matthews used to go home and tell her mother what the 'ghost' had said. She was about ten years old at the time and did not know the Bible passage quoted but she heard it so often on Sundays (and *only* on Sundays) at the haunted house, that she always remembered it. She never saw anything, just heard various sounds. Once after the reading she tried to stop the 'ghost' before it got back into the wall but the sounds ceased and the brick replaced itself.

Jim Sharratt tells me he was very puzzled by the idea that a ten-year-old child should go through such an experience without any mention of being afraid and in reply to his questions on this aspect, Mrs Tennant said: 'I was brought up on a farm in a wood; it was lovely, but I was never scared.'

During the course of an article in the *Wigan Observer* in 1969 Cyril Dickinson recalled the strange story and mentioned that the cottage, stone-built with thick walls, was over a hundred years old at the time that the disturbances took place. He says *three* of the Winstanley boys were in one bed in the oak-raftered low-ceilinged upstairs room when they heard knockings and rumblings in the walls. These noises, according to the *Wigan Observer* at the time, 'seemed to travel in the direction of a walled-in window that the exigencies of the Window Tax of the past had probably caused to be bricked up'. The window recess was used as a sort of cupboard and in it resided two large books and a number of other objects.

The noises awakened the three youths who asked who was there but this enquiry brought no response. 'Fear seized upon them and this was not at all abated when the hanging was taken from the window space and placed over their heads like a pall.' Paper and mortar was torn from the walls and scattered about the room. Stones under the window board below the window were loosened and then pulled out and thrown across the room. It was noticed early on that the disturbances always took place in darkness and only when one particular lad was present.

As news of the remarkable happenings spread, more and more people came from far and near to see and hear something of the wonders. Sure enough, as soon as the light in the 'haunted' bedroom was turned out the noises would begin and the stones – which had been replaced during the day and wedged in so tightly that they could not be removed by hand – came away by themselves and dropped to the floor or flew across the room. So great was the noise caused by the thumping of the wall-stones on to the boarded floor that people standing sixty yards away could hear it. At length the 'unseen visitant' became so aggressive that the occupants of the 'haunted room' refused to sleep there.

On more than one occasion the two weighty books, described as 'massive tomes', are said to have been thrown from the window recess halfway across the room. One, 'as large as a family Bible', was a *History of England* and the other, an ancient edition of the works of the Roman historian, Titus Livius.

It may be of interest to record the fact that the graveyard immediately below the haunted house, just across the narrow road, contained the grave of George Lyon, a notorious highwayman who was hanged in 1815 at Lancaster and whose body was brought home for burial. His grave was situated almost directly outside the disturbed house.

In a published life of George Lyon it is stated that the haunted house was 'a most ancient structure, built of stone, centuries old, and believed to have underground passages' but Jim Sharratt tells me there were no passages underneath the house although the White Lion Inn next door had two. In 1922 the haunted house was purchased by Up Holland

District Council from the owner, Mr Alec Young, and about 1927 the property was demolished, together with the Bank House opposite, the home of Miss Matthews, later Mrs Tennant, to make way for street-widening. Mr John Tennant (Mrs Tennant's husband) was at the time foreman in charge of the demolition. He noticed that the cellar beams were joined together by wooden pegs and that all the dividing walls in the upper parts of the house were composed of tree branches interlocked as in wicker-work. The plaster he described as 'lamb-stave and daub' a primitive form of plaster. Altogether it seems likely that the house was several hundred years old, but the disturbances seem to have been of a typical poltergeist character and in all probability were associated or connected (albeit unconsciously) with one or more of the youngsters in the house, although it is not impossible that a curious combination of some historical happening and adolescence combined to produce a nine days' wonder.

Wallasey, MERSEYSIDE

Leasowe Castle used to be the summer home of the fifth Earl of Derby; now it is a nurses' home. Once it was known by the curious name of Mockbegger Hall and in its time it has been a private house, a hostel for sailors, a hotel and a convalescent home for railway workers. There are reputed to be the ghosts of a man and a young boy here but who they are, why they haunt the place, or indeed if they still do so, nobody really seems to know. The ghosts of Leasowe Castle are perfect examples of unknown ghosts haunting a house for unknown reasons; perhaps it is significant in its anonymity and such apparitions are more evidential than known ghosts, who can be said to be expected to be seen by those who do see them and have little or no objective reality outside the minds of those who do so.

In the present nurses' sitting-room there is a dummy

bookcase, masking a door to a passage, now blocked up but formerly leading to a window which looked into the basement. It is the Boardroom, with its enormously thick walls, that is said to harbour the ghosts and indeed this apartment used to be called the Ghost Room.

Nearby there are three boulder stones and a local legend has it that these stones were once the favourite haunt of a fascinating but dangerous mer-maiden. To look upon her was certain death and she is said to have been seen last about the time of the turn of the century. One night when the tide was in flood and the moon was full, the sea-woman with the tail of a fish was seen combing her hair in the accustomed manner of such creatures. There is an eighteenth-century Chap-book relating in detail the experience of one John Robinson, a mariner, who saw and spoke to a mermaid here.

Liscard Castle, a fine, large and haunted house that commanded extensive marine and land views, and lived up to its name with its impressive battlements and stone lion embellishments, although it was never a castle. In the nineteenth century the property was occupied by John Astley Marsden, a prominent brush manufacturer and his imposing house was commonly referred to as 'Brush Castle'; thereafter it never lost the appendage of 'Castle'.

The ghost story associated with the house concerned a young sea captain who bought the house and took his beautiful young bride to live there. One day not long after the wedding, the captain was drowned at sea and the shock so disturbed his young wife that she immediately went out and drowned herself in a neighbouring pit, hoping to rejoin her husband of a few weeks. The pit was afterwards known as Captain's Pit. Thereafter the ghost of the sad lady is said to have haunted the house and a former resident, a master builder, is among those who have related their experiences with this ghost.

This man said that one day after he had been superintending the blocking up of some old passages in the basement, he heard a loud and persistent knocking emanating from the newly-erected brickwork after the workmen had left and thinking that somehow someone must have been inadvertently bricked up, he went close to the wall and shouted, enquiring as to who was there. He received no reply but the knocking continued and, suddenly overcome by a strange fear, he turned and ran up the steps and out into the daylight. Other residents and visitors to the house known as Liscard Castle, demolished in 1902, asserted that from time to time they heard the unaccountable sounds of a woman sobbing or they have glimpsed the shadowy form of a young woman flitting silently about the rambling house.

Warrington, CHESHIRE

Remains of the ancient Augustine Friary Church are to be seen in the local museum together with a plan and some interesting information. It is evident that the Friary and its grounds once occupied a considerable space and some idea of just how big the place was can be judged by the many places in the area whose name is prefixed by the word 'Friars'. An old house on the south side of Friars Gate, near the corner of Friars Green stood on part of the Friary Church graveyard and nearby there used to stand a low-built yellow house with a small front garden.

One summer evening when she was a child, one of the elderly occupants of this house always maintained that she was playing on the front door step when an elderly man with a bald head approached the house and passed her. She noticed that he seemed to be dressed in a curious 'long hairy frock' but he passed swiftly on into the house, not appearing to notice her. She saw him go upstairs and disappear into a large cupboard! She ran indoors and told her aunt what she had seen and the aunt, naturally somewhat alarmed, immediately went upstairs and opened wide the doors of the cupboard. It was completely empty. The house was then searched from top to bottom but no sign of the mysterious man was ever found.

One person who talked with the girl about the strange matter years later realized that she knew nothing of monks and friars but the description of the bald head and long dress could easily describe a friar; was he perhaps revisiting a place once very familiar to him?

Many years ago a house nearly opposite the old Swan Inn bore the name of Viro House and it was said to be haunted by a lady in white. The house stood on high ground with a pleasant garden sloping down to the street and the house itself, with its trailing vine, had a happy atmosphere. Who the Viro White Lady was or what she wanted nobody knows but who can blame her for returning to such lovely surroundings if she could.

Just south of Warrington, in the hamlet of Higher Walton, stands Walton Hall where each June a bathroom door is reputed to open by itself and mysteriously close without any living person being near it. There are several local stories that may account for this odd and ghostly happening including one which concerns an eighteenth-century elderly lady of the house who was almost helpless; she became ill in her bath and frantically tried to get out and obtain help but sadly she died in the bathroom that now has a haunted door.

To the north-west, near the Sankey Canal, stands Bewsey Old Hall. Part of the house was demolished some years ago but the south wing of the Hall, dating from about 1600, is at present (1977) being restored, I am informed by Mr W. B. Leeming, Divisional Librarian.

This worthy work is being carried out under the direction of the Warrington New Town Development Corporation. The property is not occupied at the time of writing but this atmospheric place was the scene of a strange little chapter in history.

In ancient days the butler of a great family was equivalent to a Comptroller or Master of the Household and such a position could only be held by a knight of good name. A descendant of the first Butler at Bewsey Hall married the heiress of Matthew Villiers, Lord of Warrington, and so became possessed of Bewsey Hall and its surrounding property, including the rights of a ferry across the Mersey, then the only communication between the Lancashire and Cheshire sides and a monopoly that brought a substantial annual income.

During the reign of Henry VII this right led to the murder of Sir John Butler, lord of the manor. The King decided to pay a visit to his stepfather, the first Earl of Derby, at Latham House. The King's itinerary would involve crossing by Sir John's ferry, a passage that would cause many hours' delay, not to mention the danger in those days of many heavily laden horses and mules, so the Earl of Derby conceived the idea of building a bridge for his royal stepson. The land on the Cheshire side belonged to him but he bought some land on the Lancashire side that belonged to a man named Norris and he built his bridge – much to the chagrin and vexation of Sir John Butler whose ferry was now rendered useless and who was thus deprived of a sizeable income.

Sir John's attitude and forthright manner of stating his views caused a quarrel to break out between him and the Earl but when the time drew near for the King's visit the Earl, anxious to be on good terms with all his neighbours when the King and his entourage were in the locality, sent a polite note to Sir John asking him whether he would like to be one of the company of Lancashire noblemen and gentlemen who were to accompany him when he went to meet the monarch. Sir John treated the invitation with contempt and sent an ungracious reply.

The Earl of Derby was an important and powerful man; he had vast possessions in Lancashire and there was also his relationship by marriage to Henry VII. Such an affront to his dignity could not be overlooked. The Earl himself may not have had any part in what followed but in the old chronicles the name of his son, Lord Stanley, is definitely given as one of the people involved: 'Sir John Butler, knight, was slaine in his bedde by the procurement of the Lord Stanley, Sir Piers Leigh and Mister William Savage joining with him in that action.'

According to legend a servant at Bewsey Hall was bribed to set a light in one of the windows at midnight to guide the murderers across the broad moat and once silently inside the Hall they were led to the sleeping chambers of Sir John, where they encountered his chamberlain, Houlcroft, guarding his master. In vain they tried bribes and inducements; the old servant was incorruptible and at length the desperate men, determined not to be thwarted at the last moment, attacked Houlcroft and succeeded in striking him to the ground. But the noise of the clash of arms and the servant's cries awakened Sir John, who leapt from his bed, only to be immediately attacked and hacked to pieces by the three murderers before he could defend himself.

Lady Butler was sleeping in the same room together with their infant son. She was spared but the desperate intruders made for the cradle intent on killing the heir to the title – but the cradle was empty. One story suggests that while Houlcroft and his master were being attacked, a faithful page crept in with a basket and whisked the child to safety at the nearby Priory of St Augustine, to be recovered by his mother next morning. As he was leaving the room the page was challenged by one of the attackers who wanted to know what was in the basket; the page replied that he had the head of his slain master and he was going to set it up on Warrington Bridge, and so he escaped. When they discovered that they had been tricked they hanged the page on a tree in the park.

The other possibility, perhaps the more credible, is that a faithful negro servant, awakened by the noise of the affray, entered the room by another door, snatched up the babe and took it to a nurse in an adjoining room; the negro then returned to Sir John's bedroom and managed to hold the murderers at bay while the nurse escaped with the child.

The negro was finally murdered but meanwhile the child was safe at the Priory.

The likelihood of the latter story being the correct one is enhanced by the fact that in what was formerly Bewsey Chapel in Warrington Church, on the alabaster tomb of Sir John and Lady Butler, there is also the figure of a negro, his body having been buried with those of his master and mistress. Whatever the truth of the matter the sounds of frantic skirmishing were periodically said to have been heard in the vicinity of Sir John's apartment and the ghostly figure of the murdered man haunted Bewsey Hall for many years.

Waterfoot, near Rochdale, GREATER MANCHESTER

The Railway Inn is said to be regularly haunted by the figure of a tall lady dressed in grey who has been reported to appear in a certain bedroom and walk through a partition wall. Known as 'Jane' by the licensees, she has been blamed for interfering with bedclothes and sometimes pulling them completely off a bed. A bricked-up room, where the only entrance is through a trapdoor in the ceiling, may possibly be associated with the haunting although as far as can be ascertained there is nothing unusual or macabre in the room now or in its past history.

West Kirby, MERSEYSIDE

The area known as Grange is reputed to harbour several ghosts. There was the ghost of old Mrs Glegg that was supposed to walk at midnight at certain times of the year in The Mount; there was said to be an unknown but frightening ghost of some kind in the narrow part of a lane between West Kirby and Caldy and another, well-known in the neighbourhood, that haunted Highfield Lane, a weird, cackling, leaping dwarf of a thing that caused the locality to be carefully avoided more than a hundred years ago. Details and the possible history and origin of these 'buggons', as they were called in the Wirral, are sadly lacking; a typical example is the rhyme about such a ghost at nearby Prenton, of which all that now remains to remind us of something that was very real to our ancestors are the two lines:

> When gorse is in blossom and holly is green,
> Prenton Hall buggon is then to be seen ...

Westhoughton, near Bolton, GREATER MANCHESTER

When Francis Lee, the former England footballer, moved into an old farmhouse at West Loughton, south-west of Bolton, stories were revived of the house on Higher Landedmans Farm being haunted.

A former occupant, Mrs Maggie Heatley, lived in the house for thirty-six years and she said she never regarded the house as haunted although there was one strange incident. It was in 1963 and both Mrs Heatley and her husband (who died in 1967) found themselves awakened in the middle of the night by what sounded like a knock on the front door and, as they listened, they heard footsteps outside the house. They got out of bed and looked out of the window but they could see nothing to account for the sounds although it was a bright, clear, moonlit night.

Next day an American who said he had been born at the house called and asked whether he could have a look round. While he was walking round the house Mrs Heatley mentioned to him their experience of the previous night. He was quite put out by the story because that night he said he had dreamed that he had called at the house.

This incident, which may well have been coincidence, was talked about in the neighbourhood and Mrs Heatley thought it might be the origin of the idea that the house was haunted. Mrs Lee agreed but said such stories did make one aware of any strange noises and she revealed that one day she and her husband were scraping one of the old beams in the house when they heard a knocking sound. It seemed to be coming from the beam they were working on; but there is a joiners' yard nearby and they decided that the noise must have come from there.

Wigan, GREATER MANCHESTER

The seventeenth-century Minorca Inn on Wallgate was reported to have a ghost in 1972 that drew beer! The manager Robert Baker, claimed that the ghost passed through locked doors and windows, interfered with apparatus such as the tape-recording machine and drew itself some beer.

In July Mr Baker had been awakened about midnight by a loud 'click' like a door being opened and then he heard creaking floorboards that suggested someone walking across the floor. Mr Baker slipped quietly into the bar but there was no one there and no sign of anyone having been there except for half a pint of beer that had been newly drawn from one of the pumps. This was particularly puzzling because all the pumps are switched off in the cellar and the cellar is always locked at night.

A few nights later exactly the same thing happened – a loud click, creaking floorboards and some beer was found to have been drawn from one of the pumps. This time Robert Baker made a careful check of the pumping system but everything appeared to be working perfectly.

Then, early one morning, at about 2.30 a.m. in fact, music suddenly flooded the establishment: the tape machine had been switched on. Yet the main electricity switch was off and only the manager had the key to that switch. One of the 'experts' consulted by Mr Baker in an effort to solve the mystery told him that there were reliable reports of ghosts in public houses but he wouldn't have expected them to drink beer! Oddly enough the beer was never consumed.

To the east once stood impressive Ince Hall, home of the Gerard family, and it is said to have been a member of this ancient lineage who died before the lawyer he had sent for arrived to make his will. It was decided to see whether the traditional dead man's hand might have the desired affect and the attorney's clerk was sent to Bryn Hall to borrow the famed 'Holy Hand'.

The hand, which still exists, belonged to Saint Edmund Arrowsmith who was executed in 1623 for his faith. Just before his death he asked one of his friends to sever a hand after his death as he was convinced that miracles would be performed through his lifeless hand. Indeed, a great many people travelled many miles and afterwards testified to the miraculous healing power of Arrowsmith's 'Holy Hand'.

The body of the dead Gerard was duly rubbed with the holy relic and the inert body apparently revived sufficiently to sign the will! After the funeral the daughter of the dead man produced an unsigned will, leaving the property to his son and daughter but the lawyer produced the will duly signed by a dead hand: a will that conveyed all the property to himself. The son, understandably, quarrelled with the lawyer; the argument developed into a fight and having struck the attorney to the ground, the son, thinking that he had killed him, hurriedly left the country and was never heard of again. Curiously enough the daughter too seems to have disappeared and the whole affair was a great mystery until, many years later, a gardener dug up a skull in a part of the grounds that were not usually cultivated; a skull that proved to be that of a young woman . . . and then the haunting long associated with Ince Hall made sense for there was a room where according to many reports a phantom and shadowy form of a young woman was seen by visitors and passers-by, hovering over the place where her remains were buried. It is said that the ghost also haunted the dishonest lawyer repeatedly, hanging suspended in the air before his eyes at the most unexpected moments and eventually he died at Wigan, full of remorse and despair.

A variation of this story casts an uncle as the bad man of the plot, depriving his nephew and niece of their rightful inheritance. When the truth was discovered the nephew strikes his uncle and, thinking he has killed him, panics and disappears abroad, never to return, while the niece's disappearance is a further mystery until a gardener digs up her skull years later. Meanwhile the ghost has often been seen at the Hall and the evil uncle goes out of his mind and spends his last years in a mental institution at Wigan.

No one really knows what it was that happened at the elegant and moated house with Corinthian columns and six sharply pointed gables that gave rise to the haunting, but if the details of the story have become confused over the centuries there is no disputing that Ince Hall was long famous for its ghost of a young girl.

Worsley, GREATER MANCHESTER

Wardley Hall is famous for its malevolent skull but legend has been piled upon legend and it is no longer possible to substantiate any of the various ancient stories. One popular tale tells of the last male of his line, one Roger Downe, earning for himself an unenviable reputation as a dissolute blade of Charles II's court; one of those whose idea of fun was to swagger about the fashionable streets of London and pick quarrels with defenceless and harmless passers-by and so have the opportunity of slitting a nose or slicing off an ear with little risk of retaliation. As a rule the 'watch', those forerunners of the police, were past their prime, feeble even, and only too ready to avoid any kind of clash with troublesome young and armed men but one night, on London Bridge, the watchman defended himself with such vigour that the head of Roger Downe was severed from his body and fell into the gutter.

Downe's sister was then living at Wardley Hall and to her

the head was despatched, packed in a box. She placed the head on the staircase where it has since remained except for the rare occasions when it has been moved – with dire consequences. The first time the head was moved was when she thought she would give the gruesome relic proper Christian burial but the very night that it was buried a terrible storm literally shook the house and all the barns and outhouses lost their roofs. Everyone at Wardley Hall was terrified and spent the awful night in various parts of the Hall that they hoped would be safe. When dawn broke, bright and still, they explored the house for damage – and found the skull back in its accustomed place on the staircase!

Over the years there were one or two other attempts at burying the relic but each time disturbances coincided with the removal of the head from the Hall and a special recess was eventually built for the head and there it has remained ever since. There is even a clause in the lease of Wardley Hall forbidding removal or concealment of the skull.

Historical fact does not substantiate the legend of Roger Downe, who was buried in Wigan churchyard and when his coffin was opened in 1799 his head was duly found still attached to his body. An alternative story suggests that the Wardley skull is that of a man named Barlow, a Roman Catholic priest who was executed in 1641 for celebrating Mass. His head was impaled on a church in Manchester, from where it is supposed to have been taken in secret to Wardley Hall where some stains in one of the bedrooms are said to be the marks of a bloody hand and foot that time cannot erase.

In February 1977 the Rev. John Allen, the Secretary of Wardley Hall, told me that there is a monograph on the Wardley Hall skull, written by the Rev. J. E. Bamber in 1970, in the Manchester Local History Library. He tells me that Canon Bamber's account is careful and scholarly; briefly it shows that the Wardley Hall skull is that of the Benedictine martyr, the same Barlow, who was born in 1585 and was hanged, drawn and quartered for his religious beliefs at Lancaster in 1641. At the time the Downe family were owners of Wardley Hall and since the Downes and the Barlows were related the Downe family brought the head of their kinsman to the Hall. The skull achieved national notoriety, Mr Allen tells me, when it was stolen in 1930. Journalists from all over the country visited the area and in seeking to obtain copy for their newspaper, were treated by the local inhabitants to some very wild stories. The skull was returned early in 1931 and has been undisturbed ever since.

Wycoller, near Colne, LANCASHIRE

Wycoller Hall is now a ruin but once it was haunted by a rustling lady and by a spectral horseman who was thought to be one of the ancient Cunliffe family, whose coat of arms is still emblazoned in the chancel windows of Whalley Church; the Cunliffe family home was at Billington, near Whalley, before Wycoller became theirs through marriage.

The spectral horseman is or was said to visit Wycoller once a year, when the wind howls and there is no moon and shadows are pools of darkness around the remains of the house on which Charlotte Brontë based Ferndean Manor in *Jane Eyre*. The rider gallops his horse up the road, over the narrow bridge, and dismounts with a curse at the door of the Hall before dashing up the wide staircase. Then the frantic screams of his wife were said to be heard, subsiding into groans. The rider returns to his horse and rides off into the dark night. The haunting is supposed to perpetuate an actual event when a Cunliffe beat his wife to death with a dog whip after seeing her in the arms of an apparent lover, but the 'lover' was only her long-lost brother and the murderous Cunliffe has to seek atonement by re-enacting his awful deed.

The rustling lady episode begins with the sound of a fox-hunt approaching the Hall. A fox, wild with panic and fatigue, races through the open door of the Hall and up the stairs. The hunt follows, horses, hounds and men bursting into the Hall, up the stairs and into a room where the lady of the house screams and screams as the dogs corner the fox and tear it to pieces. Simon Cunliffe laughs at his wife's timidity but the smile freezes on his face as she turns pale and falls to the ground at his feet, dead; the rustling of her dress as she falls ends the ghostly incident.

ILLUSTRATIONS

Skull House, Appley Bridge, a place riddled with mystery and legend surrounding a human skull.

The Appley Bridge skull, the harbinger of misfortune. It possesses the power of returning to its home by itself.

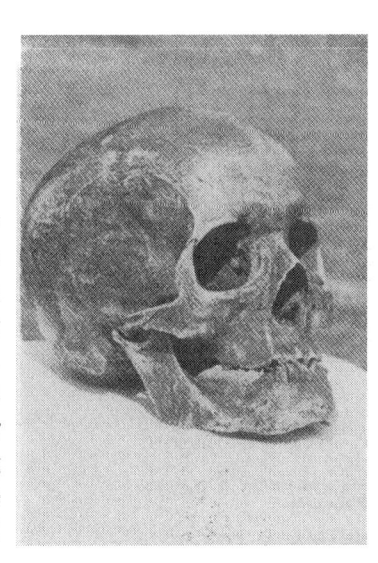

Gradwell Old Farmhouse, Croston, where the 'Scarscowe Lady' apparition once walked.

Owner Denis Mather and the author's wife outside haunted Swillbrook House, Bartle.

218

Lyme Park, Disley, has a ghostly funeral cortege and a fascinating secret hiding place.

Tower Grange, Formby. The earlier, more haunted part, is situated on the left of the picture; here a murdered priest is said to return.

Exterior and private lounge of Chingle Hall, Goosnargh, often regarded as Britain's most haunted house. The galleon motif over the fireplace once moved by itself into the centre of the room.

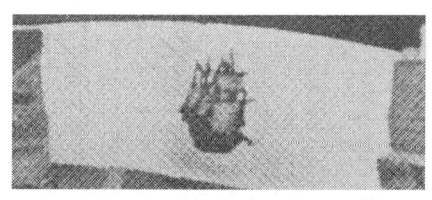

Townhouse, Littleborough, where the ghost of 'Lady Margaret' was seen in 1971.

The author examining the ancient 'Written Stone' near Longridge which is said to imprison a ghost.

Osbaldstone Hall, Ribchester, the scene of murder, everlasting bloodstains and an arresting phantom.

Some of the damage alleged to have been caused by the Runcorn poltergeist in the early 1950s.

The haunted house at Up Holland, now demolished. The haunted room was situated on the first floor above the man standing by the doorway.

Steuart Kiernander talks to Vera Bottomley at the spot in the Brushes Valley near Stalybridge where she and her cousin saw two phantom Highlanders.

Index

Accrington Hall, 10
Agincourt, Battle of, 53, 69
Ainsworth family, 37, 39
Allen, Rev. John, 212–13
Anderton, near Rivington, 150
Anderton family, 122
Anderton Hall, near Rivington, 151
Animals, awareness of ghosts, 33, 36, 42, 44, 51, 54, 63–4, 78–9, 81, 83, 95, 99, 100, 102, 107, 109, 112, 148, 165, 166, 170, 172, 179, 183–4, 186, 191
Arnold School, Blackpool, 29
Arrowsmith, Saint Edmund, 210
Arthur, King, 16
Ashton Hall, Lancaster, 115
Ashworth, William, 10
Astbury, T. J., 58
Atkinson (an architect), 81
Audenshaw, Ashton-under-Lyne, 17–18
Augustine Friary Church, Warrington, 203–4

Baker, Robert, 209
Ball, Janet, 14–15
Bamber, Rev. J. E., 212
Barlow, Alexander, 212
Barlow, Ambrose, 212–13
Barlow, Mr and Mrs Richard, 51–2
Barnside Hall, near Colne, 64, 65
Baron family, 156–7
Barrymore family, 144, 145
Barton family, 37
'Baum Rabbit' (ghost), 152–5

Beauclerk family, 182, 183
Becket family, 113
Bee, Rev. and Mrs Robert, 177–8
Bell and Bottle, Kirkham, 112
Bennet, Father, 150–1
Berry, John, 160, 164
Beswick family, 100–5
Bewsey Old Hall, near Warrington, 204–7
Bibby, John, 40
Billington, near Whalley, 213
Bingham, Michael, 92
Birch, Mrs, 97
Birchen Bower estate, 100–5
Bispham Hall, Billinge, 21
Black Abbey, Accrington, 9
Black Prince, the, 68, 69
Blackshaw, Mr and Mrs, 82
Blacon, Saltney, 175
Blighty's Club, Farnworth, 80
Boardman, William, 126
Boar's Head, Middleton, 135, 137, 138
'Bonnie' Prince Charlie, 101, 125, 185, 186
Bottomley, Vera, 183–5
Bradshaw Bridge, Bolton, 41
Bradshaw Chapel, Bolton, 45
Bradshaw family, 48–9, 133, 191
Bradshaw Hall, Bolton, 41, 45, 46, 47, 48, 49
Bramall Hall, Bramhall, 50–1
Bramshill, Hampshire, 73
Bray, Eric, 148
Brazier, Richard and Dorothy, 34–5
Breightmet, Bolton, 31
Britannia Inn, Stockport,

Britannia Inn (*contd.*)
185–6
Bromily, Ivy, 35
Bromley-Davenport, Lt Col.
  Sir Walter, 54–6
Bromley-Davenport, William,
  55
Brontë, Charlotte, 213
Brough, Robert, 40
Brownlow family, 37
Brungerley Bridge, near
  Clitheroe, 61
'Brush Castle', Wallasey, 202
Brushes Valley, Stalybridge,
  184–5
Bryn Hall, near Wigan, 210
Budworth Mere, near
  Northwich, 145
Burrill, J., 61
Butler, Sir John, 205–7
Butterworth, John, 39
Byrom, John, 175
Byron, Joseph, 37
Byron Street, Runcorn, 159–66

Caen, Battle of, 69
Cameron, D., 173
Carson, Olive, 77–9
Cartwright, Freda, 128
Cash, Mr and Mrs Donald,
  155–6
Causeway Farm, Crossens,
  Southport, 180
Chadderton, Ernest, 74–6
Chapman, Mrs, 136
Charles I, 133, 191
Charles II, 182, 211
Cheetham, Mr and Mrs Arthur,
  81–2
Cheetwood Old House,
  Cheetwood, 101, 102
Chingle Hall, Goosnargh,
  88–93
Churchdown shore, Southport,
  181

City Hospital, Chester, 59
Civil War, 16, 19, 52, 72,
  138, 139, 144
Classic Cinema, Accrington,
  10–11
Classic Cinema, Bury, 54
Clayton Hall, Droylsden, 71
'Clayton Hall Boggart', 71
Clifton, Squire John Talbot,
  122–3
Cliviger Gorge, Burnley, 52
Cohen, David (Investigation
  Officer, Manchester Psychical
  Research Society), 135,
  136, 156, 157
Collinson, Albert, 108–9
Collyhurst, Manchester, 130
Colne Hall, Colne, 63–4
Colverley, Brian, 130
Combermere Abbey, Nantwich,
  141–2
Commercial Hotel, Radcliffe,
  149–50
Conchie, Ethel, 113
Congleton, near Macclesfield,
  54
Connolly, Chris, 125
Conservative Club, Disley, 70
Corbridge, Hannah, 64–5
Cottam Hall, 111
Crank, near St Helens, 166–70
Cromwell, Oliver, 16, 20,
  132, 137, 138
Croppers Hill, St Helens, 166
Crosby, Merseyside, 176
Crossens, Southport, 180–1
Crowther, Mr and Mrs Harold,
  164–6
Crumpsall Hospital, Manchester,
  129–30
Cunliffe, C. W., 73
Cunliffe family, 213–14
Cyclic ghosts, 36–7, 40, 50,
  52, 60, 65, 111, 157, 175

Dabbs, Richard, 151-2
Dale, Joseph, 70
Dane Road Railway Station, Manchester, 128
Danyers family, 69
Daulman, Rev. John H., 129, 130
Davenport, William, 51
Davenport Theatre, Stockport, 189
Davies, John, 107
Davies, Trevor, 32
Davis, Ann and Andre, 107-8
Davis, Mr (a publican), 164
Day, James Wentworth, 93
de Hoghton family, 58
de Lea, Sir Henry, 58
De Quincey, Thomas, 101, 102
de Trafford family, 19-20
Deane, Bolton, 37
del Ton family, 116
Dennis, Mrs, 34
Derby family, 38, 201, 205-7
Dickinson, Cyril, 199
Dimond, Rev. Edward, 175
Dodd, Ken, 118-19
Downe, Roger, 211-13
Drinkwater, Philip, 12
Driver, Betty and Freda, 132-3
Dunham Park, Altrincham, 15
Dunkenhalgh, Clayton-le-Moors, 59-61
'Dunkley Boggart', 60
Dunleavy, Bernadette and Brian, 147-8
Dunnet, Sally, 173
Dunshaw College, Leyland, 116
Dyson, Ted, 127

Eagles Crag, Cliviger Gorge, 52
Earl Hall, near Colne, 65
Easton, Reginald, 196-7
Edward II, 58
Edward III, 53
Egan, Lynn, 32
Egerton Hall, near Bolton, 74-6
Elcho, Lord, 186
Elizabeth I, 72, 86, 94, 111, 159
Evans, Mrs, 90
Everlasting bloodstains, 28, 150
Exorcism, 24, 30, 31, 35, 72, 107, 114, 130, 174, 175
Eyam, 70

Fancy Lodge, Hey Houses, 100
Farndon Bridge, Farndon, 79
Ferguson, Mary, 40
'Ferndean Manor', 213
Ferranti Factory, Hollinwood, 100, 105
Few family, 58
Finch, Thomas, 111
Fitton, Mary, 84, 86, 87, 88
Fleet Prison, London, 86
Fleetwood family, 79, 181
Fleming, Edward, 156
Formby Hills beach, 83
Fox, John, 71
Franz Joseph, Emperor of Austria, 96
Fryer, Alfred, 70

Garlick, Canon Wilfred, 191-3
Garnock, Lady, 142
Gawsworth Church, Gawsworth, 87
Gawsworth Hall, Gawsworth, 84-8
Gawsworth Old Rectory, Gawsworth, 85-8
George IV, 180
George and Dragon, Chester,

George and Dragon (*contd.*) 58–9
Gerard family, 210–11
Ghost Club, The, 146
'Ghost House', Up Holland, 197–201
Ghost photographs (alleged), 142, 186
Gibbons, Grinling, 68
Gilbert, W. S., 186
Gill family, 112–13
Girl Guides Association, 63
Gleaves, Frances, 36
Glegg family, 196
Glen, Dr Donald, 157
Glynn, Eileen, 160
Glynn, John, 160–4
Glynn, Major and Mrs J. M., 72, 73
Glynn, M. K., 193
Golborne, near Newton-le-Willows, 143
Gorsey Bank, Stockport, 187–8
Gorton, Manchester, 128
Gournell, Sidney, 11
Gradwell family, 66–7
Grant, Alex, Chairman, Kirkby Local History Society, 114–15
Grant, Dave, 12
Gratton, William, 109
Great Budworth, near Northwich, 145
Green Lady, 20
Gresty, Dorothy, 172–3
Grey Ladies, 55, 75, 158–9, 207
Griffiths' Mill, Chester, 59
Guide to Rochdale, 153
Gun Hill, Bosley, 40–1
Gwynn, Nell, 182

Hale Barns Green, 94
Hale Low Farm, Hale, 93–4
Hall-i-th'-Wood, Bolton, 36–7
Hambridge, Colonel, 48
Hamburger, Sidney, 129
Hamill, Chris, 113–14
Handley, Rev. Neil, 31
Hanson, Mr and Mrs Derek, 81, 82
Hardcastle, Colonel Henry M., 41–2, 47
Hargreaves, Frank, 11
Hargreaves family, 12, 13, 14
Harlick, Mrs, 136
Harpurhey Cemetery, Manchester, 104
Harrington, Earls of, 85
Harrington Arms, Gawsworth, 86
Harrison, Stan, 147
Harrison family, 183–4
Harrop, Janet, 96
Hartley, Christopher, 64
Haselwell family, 196
Haydock, George, Vivian and William, 111
Headless Cross, near Rivington, 150
Heath Cross, Crewe, 66
Heatley, Maggie, 208–9
Heaton family, 122
Henry V, 53
Henry VII, 205
Henry VIII, 93
Herbert, William, 86
Hesketh family, 79, 158–9, 181–2
Heskin Hall, Eccleston, 72–3
Heywood, Mr and Mrs John, 43–5
Heywood, Thomas, 187
Higginbotham, Mary and Robert, 190–1
Higgins, Kevin, 149
Higgins, Lily, 187–8
Higher Bebington, Birkenhead, 25

Higher Landedmans Farm, West Loughton, 208–9
Higher Walton, near Warrington, 204
Highwayman Horrocks, 30
Hill, Joe, 151
Hill Presbytery, Goosnargh, 93
Hippodrome Theatre, Altrincham, 11
History of England, 200
Hobgoblins, 83
'Holy Hand', 210
Hopkins, Matthew, 'witchfinder general', 168
Hopwood family, 138
Hormby, Catherine, 51
Horwich, near Rivington, 151
Howarth, Harold, 116–17
Howarth, Mayard, 89–92
Hull, 92
Hulley family, 17–18
Hutton, Battle of, 53
Hyde Lads Club, Hyde, 107–8

Imperial Chemical Industries, 144
In Search of Ghosts, 93
In Search of the Supernatural, 91
Ince Hall, near Wigan, 210–11
Institute of Technology, Bolton, 34
Irwell Castle Hotel, Salford, 173–4

Jackson, Annabel Huth, 39
Jackson, Mary and Bob, 187
James I, 168
Jane Eyre, 213
Jenks, Fred, 126–7
Jepson, Mr and Mrs, 90
John, King, 28, 37

Johnson, Samuel 'Maggotty', 85
Johnstone, Harold, 36
Jones, C., 24–5
Jones, K. R., 175–6
Jones, Lucy, 160–1
Jones, Samuel, 160–5

Kersal Cell, Salford, 175
Kevill, Martin H., 67
Kiernander, Freda and Steuart, 42, 132, 135, 136, 170, 183
King, Ned (highwayman), 106–7
Kingsley, Runcorn, 164
Kirkholt, Rochdale, 156–7
Knight of the Death's Head, 16
Knight of the Skull, 16
Knights Templars, 37
Knollys, Sir William, 86
Knotty Ash, Liverpool, 118–19

Labour Club, Wood Street, Bolton, 34–5
Lake Burwain, Foulridge, 83
Lancaster Castle, 28, 38
Lancaster Golf Club, 115
Lane End House, Mawdesley, 111
Laneshaw Bridge, near Colne, 64–5
Lathorn House, 38
Lawson, P. W. G., 182–3
Layton, Blackpool, 28–9
Leasowe Castle, Wallasey, 201–2
Lee, Mr and Mrs Francis, 208–9
Lee, H., 16
Leek, Carnforth, 57
Leeming, W. B., 204
Lees family, 71–2
Legh of Lyme family, 69

229

Leicester Street, Northwich, 143
Leigh, Sir Piers, 206
Lever, William (Lord Leverhulme), 34, 118
Leverhulme, Lord, see Lever, William
Leveson, Sir Richard, 86
Leycester family, 93–4
Linakin family, 181
Liscard Castle, Wallasey, 202–3
Little Sutton, Ellesmere Port, 77
Lomas, Tom, 43–4
London Bridge, London, 211
London Hospital, The, 146
Lostock Tower, near Bolton, 122
Lyceum Theatre, Crewe, 66
Lyme Hanly, 69
Lyme Park, Disley, 67–70
Lynch, Colin, 143, 144
Lyon, George, 200
Lytham Hall, Lytham-St-Annes, 123

Macclesfield, Earls of, 85
MacDonald, Malcolm, 34–5
MacGregor, Alasdair Alpin, 183
McKay, Mrs, 90
McLachlan, Mrs, 146–7
McLean, Carol, 119–20
McLeish family, 130–1
McSorley, Dominic, 12, 13
Madoc, Prince of Wales, 79
Makinson, Janet, 91
Manchester Airport, 126
Manchester Local History Library, 212
Manchester Natural History Museum, 104
Manor of Gawsworth, The, 87
Marbury Dunne, 145

Marbury family, 144–7
Marbury Hall, near Northwich, 144–7
Marbury Park, near Northwich, 144
Marple Hall, Marple, 133, 191
Marsden, John Astley, 202
Marsh, Rev. George, 37–8
Marwell Hall, Hampshire, 73
Mather, Denis G., 18–19
Maycock, Jeff, 76–7
Mayfield Railway Station, Manchester, 126–8
Mearnd, Josie, 24
Meaux, Battle of, 69
Medlar-with-Wesham, near Kirkham, 111
Mee, Arthur, 38
Melia family, 113
Meols Hall, Southport, 181–2
Mer-maiden, 202
Miller, Sir Geoffrey Christie, 192
Middleton Botanical Society, 137
Middleton Church, Middleton, 138, 141
Millward, Enid, 186–7
Minorca Inn, Wigan, 209–10
'Mistletoe Bough Chest', 73
Mockbegger Hall, Wallasey, 201
Mohan, Brian, 189–90
Monaco Club, Farnworth, 80
Moorby, Mrs, 90
Morgan Place, Heaton Norris, 99
Morriss, Frank, 114–15
Mortimer, Roger, 79
Mossock Hall Farm, Bickerstaffe, 20
Mottram, Longdendale, 108–10
Movey, Charlie, 127

Mowbreck Hall, near Kirkham, 111–12
Mueller, Madame, 171
Murphy, John, 10

Naden, John, 40–1
New Theatre, Crewe, 66
Normansell, Ray, 188–90
Norris, Mary, 182
Northover, Alice, 156
Norton, Les, 171–2
Nugent family, 113

O'Connell, Irene, 54
Old Rossall Hall, Fleetwood, 79–80
Old Schools Cottages, Bromley Cross, 51–2
Oldham Church, Oldham, 147
Oliver, Dr, 104
Osbaldeston family, 150
Osbaldeston Hall, near Ribchester, 150
Otterspool, Stockport, 191
Overs Houses Farm, Turton, 46
Owen, Dr George, 55, 56
Owen, Idris W., 86
Owen, Nicholas, 89
Owen's College, Manchester, 104

Palace Hotel, Birkside, 178–9
Park Hall, Charnock Richard, 58
Parkgate, near Neston, 142
Payne, Carol, 94–6
Peacock, Mrs, 140
Pearson, Fred, 63–4
Pedley, John, 14
Pedley, Kathleen, 14
Peel, Jonathan, 10
Peel Park, Accrington, 10
Peg o'Nell, 61–3
Pennystone, Mable (May), 139
Perrins, Tom, 94
Perrott, Tom, Chairman of The Ghost Club, 146
Petre family, 60, 61
Phantom nun, 25
Phillips, Aubrey, 172–3
Phoenix, Pat, 170–1
Photographs of ghosts (alleged), 76–7
Piers, Dick, 168–70
Polewhale, Captain William, 86
Poltergeist Over England, 41–2
Potter, Mabel, 130, 131
Poulton Hall, Birkenhead, 25
Powell, Frank, 35
Prenton Hall, West Kirby, 208
Pressick, A., 195–6
Price, Harry, 41–2, 47
Princess of Norway, 63
Pritchard, Cath and Colin, 187–8
Proctor, Mrs, 89
Pullen, Mr (a farmer), 168–70
Punch Bowl Inn, Hurst Green, 106–7
Punch Bowl Inn, Sefton, 176–7

Quay House, Parkgate, Neston, 142–3

Radcliffe Arms, Oldham, 147–8
Radcliffe family, 121
Radclyffe family, 37
Railway Inn, Waterfoot, 207
Ratcliffe, H. B., 159
Rectory Farm, Crossens, Southport, 180
Red Bridge, Bolton, 32
Reynolds, Kay, 117
Richards, Raymond and Monica,

Richards (*contd.*)
84–8
Riddings Road, Altrincham, 14
Ridgway, Charles, 108
Rigby, Colonel, 72
Rigby, Mrs, 91
Rigby, Stewart, 188, 189
Rigg, Hubert R., 53
Rimmer, B., 180
Ring o' Bells, Middleton, 135–40
Rishton family, 60
Rivington, Liverpool, 118
Rivington Castle (ruins), 151–2
Roberts, R. O., 59
Robertson, William, 153
Robinson, John, 202
Robinson, Mrs, 90
Rodger, Stuart, 108
Roper-Richards family, 85
Roscow, Peter, 29
Rossall Hall, 181
Rostherne Mere, near Altrincham, 157–8
Royal Hotel, Hoylake, 105–6
Royal Pavilion Cinema, Blackpool, 28
Rufford Old Hall, Rufford, 158–9
Runcorn poltergeist, 159–66
Runshaw Hall, Leyland, 116
Runshaw House, Leyland, 115–16
Ryan, Catherine and Ernest, 135–6

Sadler, George, 20
St George's Vicarage, Stockport, 191–3
St James's Church, Broughton, 175
St James's Palace, London, 68
St John the Evangelist Church, Breightmet, 31
St Mary's Church, Rochdale, 152–5
St Mary's Hospital, Manchester, 104
St Nicholas Church, Liverpool, 115
St Stephen's Church, Bolton, 31
St Thomas's Hospital, Stockport, 193–4
Sale, Cheshire, 102, 103
Saltney Junction Railway Station, 175–6
Samlesbury Hall, Blackburn, 26–8
Sankey Canal, Warrington, 204
Sarcowe Lady (ghost), 66–7
Savage, William, 206
Schofield, Robert, 149
Secret hiding places and passages, 16, 58, 66, 68, 72, 82, 89, 90, 91–2, 137, 138, 147, 186, 207
Shakespeare, Sir Geoffrey, 86
Shakespeare, William, 85, 86
Shakespeare Tavern, Manchester, 124–5
Shambles Inn, Chester, 124
Sharratt, Jim, 197–201
Sharrock, Father, 72
Shaw, Francis, 125
Ship and Royal, Lytham, 122–3
Shone, Rev. Alan, 152–5
Sidney, Lord, 182
'Sir Gareth and Lynette', 16
Skagen Court, Bolton, 35
Skull House, Appley Bridge, 15–17
Skull House Farm, 45
Skulls and hauntings, 15–17, 42–50, 210, 212–13
Sloane, Father Joseph, 130
Smethurst, Jack, 149

Smith, Bill, 185
Smith, Edna and Ronnie, 32-3
Smith, Joseph, 178-9
Smith, Malcolm, 17
Smith-Barry family, 144, 145
Smithills Hall, Halliwell, Bolton, 37-9
Social Services Hostel, Bolton, 30-1
Society for Psychical Research, 162
Somerset, 16
Southworth, Lady Dorothy, 26-8
Southworth, Sir John, 26, 28
Sowerbutts, Grace, 26
Speke Hall, Speke, 182-3
Squiers, Glanville, 68
Staining Hall, Blackpool, 28
Stainlawe, Abbot of, 81
Staircase Café, Stockport, 186-7
Stanhope family, 85
Stanley, Margaret, 21, 24
Stannycliffe family, 137-8
Stannycliffe Hall, near Middleton, 137, 138
Stark, Robert, 125-6
Stevens, Rev. W. H., 162-6
Stockport Express, 97, 188, 189, 193, 194
Stockport Grammar School, 189
Stonyhurst College, 107
Stork Hotel, Billinge, 20-1
Strickland, Ann, 91
Strickland, William, 91
Stubley Old Hall, 117
Studio One Cinema, Altrincham, 11-14
Swan Inn, Warrington, 204
Swillbrook House, Bartle, 18-19
Sykes family, 133-4

Sykes Lumb Farm, near Blackburn, 133-4

Tabley Old Hall, Plumley, 149
Tattum, Wilfred, 193
Taylor, Sir Charles, 55
Tedbury Close, Southdene, Kirkby, 112-15
Tennant, Mr and Mrs J., 198-201
Tennyson, Alfred Lord, 16
Thatched House Inn, Stockport, 187
Thorpe, Jeremy, MP, 192
Thurstaston Hall, Thurstaston, 196-7
Timberbottom case, 41-50
Timperley, Altrincham, 14
Titus Livius, 200
Tiverton, Cheshire, 195
Toby Inn, Edgworth, 76-7
Top o' th' Moss, Breightmet, 31
Tower Grange, Formby, 80-2
Tower House, Formby, 81-2
Tower of London, 111
Towneley family, 52-3
Towneley Hall, Burnley, 52-3
Townhouse, Littleborough, 116-17
Trafford Park, Manchester, 126
'Trash' (ghost), 83
Travis, Rev. Peter, 91
Turner, Colonel R. G., 196-7
Turton Moors, Bolton, 51
Turton Tower, Bolton, 47-8, 49-50

Unilevers, 118
Unsworth, E. A., 15

Van Brandt, Tessa, 136
Vanstone, Rev. W. H., 157

Vavasour Hotel, Rochdale, 155–6
Vernon Park Museum, Stockport, 186
Victoria Theatre, Salford, 172–4
Victorian Childhood, A, 39
Villiers, Matthew, Lord of Warrington, 205
Viro House, Warrington, 204

Waddow Hall, Clitheroe, 61–3
Walker, Doris and Bert, 49–50
Walker, Moira E., 63
Wall, John, 88–9
Walmeley, Mrs, 90
Walmesley family, 60, 61
Walton Hall, Higher Walton, 204
Wardley Hall, Worsley, 211–13
Warren, Earl of, 79
Warrington Bridge, Warrington, 206
Warrington Church, Warrington, 207
Watson, Frank, 160–1
Watson, Jack, 139
Watt family, 182, 183
West Hill School, Stalybridge, 183–4
Westby family, 111–12
Westminster Abbey, London, 191
Whaley Bridge, near Disley, 70, 189
Whalley Abbey, 81, 82

Whinney Heys, Layton, Blackpool, 28–9
Whirity, Mandy, 31
White, Dr Charles, 101, 102, 103, 104
White Ladies, 9, 27, 58, 69, 72, 100, 115, 116, 123, 143, 145, 148, 172–3, 182, 193–4, 204
White Lion Inn, Up Holland, 197, 200–1
White Rabbit of Crank (ghost), 167–70
Whitmore family, 196
Whittle, Ellen, 160
Wickham, Florence, 74, 76
Wilding, Peggy, 176
Wilkinson, James, 151
Wilmslow, near Macclesfield, 54
Wilshaw, George, 98–100
Winnington Bridge, Northwich, 143
Winstanley family, 198–9
Wood, William, 70
Worcester, 88
Wrights' Arms Inn, Offerton, 190
Written Stone, The, 120–1
Wycoller Hall, Wycoller, 213–14

Ye Old Rock House, Barton-on-Irwell, 19–20
Young, Alec, 201

Zenton Priory, Salford, 175

Printed in Great Britain
by Amazon